THE
PRIVATE JOURNAL
OF
F. S. LARPENT,
JUDGE-ADVOCATE GENERAL OF THE BRITISH FORCES
IN THE PENINSULA
ATTACHED TO THE HEAD-QUARTERS OF
LORD WELLINGTON DURING THE PENINSULAR WAR,
FROM 1812 TO ITS CLOSE

VOLUME III

Elibron Classics
www.elibron.com

Elibron Classics series.

© 2006 Adamant Media Corporation.

ISBN 1-4021-8870-6 (paperback)
ISBN 1-4212-9605-5 (hardcover)

This Elibron Classics Replica Edition is an unabridged facsimile
of the edition published in 1853 by Richard Bentley, London.

PRIVATE JOURNAL.

THE

PRIVATE JOURNAL

OF

F. S. LARPENT, ESQ.,

JUDGE ADVOCATE GENERAL OF THE BRITISH FORCES
IN THE PENINSULA.

ATTACHED TO THE HEAD-QUARTERS OF
LORD WELLINGTON DURING THE PENINSULAR WAR,
FROM 1812 TO ITS CLOSE.

EDITED
BY SIR GEORGE LARPENT, BART.

IN THREE VOLUMES.
VOL. III.

LONDON:
RICHARD BENTLEY, NEW BURLINGTON STREET,
Publisher in Ordinary to Her Majesty.
MDCCCLIII.

CONTENTS OF VOLUME III.

PRIVATE JOURNAL,

&c.

CHAPTER I.

MOVEMENTS OF THE ARMY—NARROW ESCAPE OF WELLINGTON —ANECDOTE OF WELLINGTON AT RODRIGO—NOVEL SCALING LADDERS — SIR ALEXANDER DICKSON — WELLINGTON'S VANITY—OPERATIONS RESUMED—SPANISH OFFICERS—THE PASSAGE OF THE ADOUR—THE ROAD TO BAYONNE—DEATH OF CAPTAIN PITTS.

Head-Quarters, St. Jean de Luz, Tuesday,
February 22nd, 1814.

MY DEAR M——

As the movements going on give me now a little more leisure, and I know not how soon my opportunities of writing may in a great measure be arrested by a march, I begin my weekly despatch early this week, and write, although really almost too cold to hold my pen. Lord Wellington, when he returned from driving the

French across the Gave, found his expedition here could not leave port from bad wind and tide, &c., though all ready. He instantly set about new arrangements in consequence, so as to be independent in a great measure of the result of this grand bridge.

All the divisions of the army, therefore, moved towards the right yesterday, except the Guards and the rest of the first division, which remain in our front backed by a corps of Spaniards at Guethany and Bidart, in advance of St. Jean de Luz, but through which place they did not march. To superintend this movement Lord Wellington was off again yesterday for Garris, near to St. Palais, with most of the head-quarters staff, the Adjutant-general Pakenham remaining here on account of a slight bilious attack.

The last move left us in front of the Gave, the French still strong in Sauveterne and on a ridge of hills and strong ground which runs between the two Gaves d'Oleron and Pau. We are now, I conclude, to drive them across both Gaves, and then make good our way round to the other side of the Adour and the citadel of Bayonne. In the meantime, as the plan here is still expected to take effect to-morrow morning early, we are all alive; our little bay full of shipping and small ships of war, which cruise backwards and forwards, or anchor there, with carpenters, sappers, soldiers, &c., on board, and all the flotilla ready in Sacoa, and the Admiral superintending.

Head-quarters are come home delighted with the country on the Gaves and with their reception. The people in many instances come in numbers to meet our troops instead of offering resistance. The prisoners also, many of them say they are ready to serve *son Altesse Royale,* but this is rather too soon to begin, it is thought, as it may be only to escape and return to their old army.

One young man, who was of the country, ran into his father's house as they were marching by, and all the family were found around him. He was separated and marched off; but the story has been told at head-quarters, and General Pakenham has sent the man back (who was on his way to Passages), and means to send him home to his friends.

I was talking to General Pakenham yesterday on beginning a French royalist corps out of the prisoners and deserters. It must be done very cautiously, of course, at first, but would, I think, have a good effect and soon increase. At present the idea that all deserters must be sent away from their own country to England, deters many from deserting, who would otherwise be willing. This object would also do away with the disgraceful ideas naturally attached to desertion to an enemy in a soldier's mind.

Reports say Lord Wellington had a narrow escape with his staff, whilst reconnoitring on the right in the late move. He is said to have been going up a hill when a French cavalry regiment was coming up the other side. The engineer officer was going round, and he saw the regiment and galloped back to give information, but before he could reach Lord Wellington they were just close to the top of the hill, and Colonel Gordon, who was in the advance, saw some of the French videttes close; he gave the alarm, and they all had a gallop for it, pursued by some of the Dragoons.

Though the English horses were most of them well tired, they were soon out of reach of the French, and all escaped. Lord Wellington confides almost too entirely in the fleetness and excellence of his animals, considering what the loss would be if he were caught; he is, however, now rather more cautious.

I heard a few days since an anecdote about the siege of Rodrigo, which shows the man. Scarcely any one knew what was to be done; the great preparations were all made in Almeyda, and most supposed, and I believe the French, that everything which arrived there, was for the purpose of defence there, not of attack elsewhere. On a sudden the army was in front of Rodrigo. A new advanced work was discovered, which must be taken before any progress could be made in the siege. To save men and time, an instant attack was resolved upon. Scaling-ladders were necessary: the engineers were applied to; they had none with them, for they were quite ignorant of the plans—an inconvenience which has often arisen in different departments from Lord Wellington's great secresy, though the general result, assisted by his genius, has been so good. The scaling could not take place without ladders; Lord Wellington was informed of this. " Well," says he, " you have brought up your ammunition and stores, never mind the waggons, cut them all up directly, they will make excellent ladders—there you see, each

side piece is already cut." This was done, and by
the help of these novel ladders, the work was
scaled forthwith.

At Badajoz, he found so little to be had in the
regular way for a siege, from want of transport,
and so many difficulties in consequence from the
regular bred artillery generals, &c., that he became
principal engineer himself, making use of Colonel
Dickson, the acting man, as his instrument. These
sieges procured Dickson his majority and lieu-
tenant-colonelcy in consequence, and though only
a Captain in the Royal Regiment of Artillery, he
now conducts the whole department here, because
he makes no difficulties.

In one instance Lord Wellington is not like
Frederick the Great. He is remarkably neat,
and most particular in his dress, considering his
situation. He is well made, knows it, and is
willing to set off to the best what nature has
bestowed. In short, like every great man, present
or past, almost without exception, he is vain. He
cuts the skirts of his own coats shorter, to make
them look smarter : and only a short time since I
found him discussing the cut of his half-boots, and
suggesting alterations to his servant, when I went

in upon business. The vanity of great men shows itself in different ways, but I believe always exists in some shape or other.

February 22nd, 5 o'clock.—The flotilla has just got out of Sacoa Bay in preparation for to-morrow. A beautiful sight ! Six or seven ships of war, and fifty other vessels—every one alive ! Forty form the bridge ; I hope it may succeed, many doubt it.

P.S.—Lord Wellington moving on the Gaves with seven divisions. The cable bridge is in the boats, engineers on board. The affair to begin by driving in the pickets, then crossing five hundred men on the rafts, spiking the French battery, burning the French corvette, and then bringing in the bridge !

February 24th, 1814.—I rose at half-past four, to go over and see the crossing of the Adour yesterday, and the formation of the bridge. At day-light I discovered the whole flotilla had been dispersed by the gale of the night before, and no part was near the mouth of the Adour. Several officers returned in consequence, saying nothing could be done ; thinking otherwise, and that this movement would somehow take place, being connected with Lord

Wellington's on our right on the Gaves, I went on, found all the Spaniards on the road in front of Bayonne, but doing nothing. All was quiet for a very long time; about twelve o'clock they were ordered to move on, and make a feint, and an attack was made by our great guns and rockets at the same time, on the French armed corvette and gun-boats, to destroy the latter, and at the same time to draw off the attention of the French from the mouth of the river below Anglet, where we intended to cross on the rafts.

The Spaniards were not much opposed, and went on boldly enough, as far as intended, and had a few wounded. The sharp-shooting, however, was very slack. The fifth division at the same time, made a show on their side, between the Nivé and the Adour, but not with any serious intention. I then went into an empty house with Dr. Macgregor and some others, to make a fire and get some breakfast, which they had with them; we added our several stocks, and fared very well. We then made our way through Anglet, and across the sands, and through a pine wood, to the river's mouth. A brigade of Guards, another of the King's German Legion, the Light Battalion, (most excellent men,) and a Rocket Brigade, were there, all ready to pass, but from the immense difficulties which had been met with in the transport of the boats and pontoons over land, only two of the light companies were over about one o'clock, when I arrived, and a temporary suspension of the passage of men had been ordered by General Hope.

The order, however, had just come again to pass over as fast as possible, and before I went away from the spot (about three o'clock) three rafts, formed each upon three pontoons, and carrying each about fifty or fifty-five men, were at work ferrying across on a cable, and the six small boats were also plying, so that about five hundred men were then nearly over, and they were going at the rate of two hundred or two hundred and fifty per hour. I left the rocket men, each with one rocket ready in his hand, and three on his back in a case, with three poles on his shoulder, just going to cross.

Elphinstone had been quite in despair; the pontoon cars sunk so much in the sand, that at last thirty horses would not move them, and for the last five hundred yards they were conveyed on the shoulders of the guardsmen; twenty-six men

to a pontoon. At length all his difficulties were
thus overcome, and the non-arrival of the bridge,
of which we could see nothing, was not his fault,
but that of the weather.

I helped the engineering again, a little, by
joining the party who were finding the best place
to which to fix cables against high-water—as I
discovered the last tide mark in the sands, and
thus found a landing-place and post, clearly above
high-water mark—as the springs were past, and of
course every succeeding tide would rise to a less
height. We then proceeded along the river towards
our battery on the bank, which was firing at the
corvette, &c. When we had gone a little way
through the pine wood, we found all the roads
almost stopped by the trees cut down by the
French, and the road we took near the bank which
was clear, carried us opposite a smaller French
corvette and three gun-boats, which had just
placed themselves in the river. At first we
thought them a part of our intended bridge, but
soon found it otherwise, and that we should be
fired at, as our small party on the other side the
river, had not advanced, and all the opposite bank
and village, as well as the boats, were still French.

We turned, and at last made our way through to the battery. We there learnt that the guns and rockets had sunk one gun-boat, and frightened away the rest, and the corvette, which had all been hauled up close to the bridge under Bayonne, where we saw them.

I could not understand that the rockets had done more than cause some alarm, though twelve had been fired at once at the shipping, and from no great distance. Only one, or at most two, had fairly struck, and nothing had been burnt. The heavy guns had struck the corvette, but could not do much damage before she was off, and just at first the corvette and battery on the French side seem to have had the best of it. Count Damas, who was there with the Duc d'Angoulême, looking on, told me that the artillery had knocked off the colours of the corvette whilst he was there, and that one of the light Germans had jumped into the water, had fetched out the colours, and had presented them to the commanding artillery officer. Others say these colours were on the gun-boat. The French were so alarmed at the rockets, that the vessel, when struck, was abandoned.

Close to our guns we found the other brigade of

Guards, &c., making an immense fire with the fir-
trees, which had been cut down on all sides, as the
day, though fine, was very cold. Dr. Macgregor,
one or two others, as well as myself, went up a
little sand-hill near, just to look round, when a
twenty-four pound shot from Bayonne came close
to us point blank. The horses turned right round,
and the Doctor losing his hat, I thought at first
that he had been struck. Of course we soon beat
a retreat, and found we were in a spot where this
was the usual reception, and a position of which
the French were jealous.

Just as I came away, a little before five, I saw
a column of French, apparently about seven hundred, going very quickly through the wood on the
opposite bank from the citadel, towards our men
who had passed, to attack them. I knew we had
nearly a battalion across, about seven hundred
men, and did not feel much alarm at the event.
I pitied the men more for the cold night they
were likely to pass on the bare sands, without
baggage, &c. I have heard this morning an
attack was made just afterwards, but that some of
the rocket skirmishers were put in advance with
the other skirmishers on our side, and the French

were so alarmed that, though much superior, they
would not advance, and our men beat them off.

The flotilla was this morning collected near the
mouth of the Adour, and, I suppose, before this
the bridge is begun. At any rate we could have
crossed as many men as we wished before this.
No one is returned to-day as yet, and as I had
business, and one of my horses was a little sore in
the back, I staid at home. My grey pony started
before six yesterday morning, and I was not at
home till past seven at night, having ridden above
thirty miles, and given him nothing to eat, but he
is not the least the worse for it to-day, as far as I
can judge now.

Some of the Spanish regiments were very fine
men, and well equipped in every respect, much
better than some of our poor fellows; but the
officers looked very bad indeed, and when the men
advanced they were led on by their officers with
cloaks on, folded over their mouths, looking as
miserable as possible.

The men also (like the French) always march
with their great coats on over everything, so that
our good new clothes were all concealed by their
own old threadbare coats. On the other hand,

you saw none of our men with their coats on, cold as it was, and every one alive and in activity. I stood next to Don Carlos d'Espagne, and heard him receive his directions and information as to what parts we occupied and what the French, &c. General Hope (though not well, and too soon, I believe) came on to take the command, of which the division were very glad.

I fear the Spaniards, though better than they were, and though only the best were in advance, will soon begin to do mischief. As I returned here I saw all their stragglers about the houses near the road, and telling every one that in Spain *Francesi roban & rompen todos todos.* They soon dirty our new clothing, and go about with dirty and scowling discontented faces, like some of our good countrymen in Ireland. The industry of the French on the sand-banks had been very great in the cultivation of the vine. The south-east side of the very bank on which the sea beat on the north-west, a pure white sand, was divided with square reed enclosures, and covered with vines. The Anglet wine (which, as a very light wine, is in repute), I believe, is there produced. Many of the inhabitants at Anglet, &c., remained, and most seemed glad the movement was over. One old woman, in a house that was near the river's mouth, said she was most happy to see us, as she had been the last two months in complete misery, not allowed to speak to any strangers by the French, and not even allowed to go to Bayonne to buy a few sous-worth of snuff. I suppose they feared the spread of information, as this was close to the intended spot of our bridge, of which I understand, and have no doubt, they had a very clear knowledge. Two persons of the better class have come in here by sea from Bordeaux, round by Passages, to pay their respects, and give information to *son Altesse Royale*. Colonel La Fitte told me they were as anxious there for Lord Wellington as the Jews were for the Messiah, so sanguine are the émigrés.

February 26th.—All accounts now agree that the French have from ten thousands to above eleven thousands in the town and citadel, three thousands in the latter, the rest in the town and lines. Another show was made against our people the morning after they crossed, but no attack. Considering the French had eleven thousand men, that it was eight or nine hours before we had above

five or six hundred men across, this passage of the
Adour and our establishment on the right bank is
most disgraceful to their troops, or to their General,
and as creditable to us. In the evening of the
24th our flotilla crossed the bar and got into the
Adour over a most tremendous surf. Several
accidents ensued in consequence, and many lives
were lost ; some say as many as forty in the whole,
of all nations. I believe about fifteen English
sailors. None but the latter would have dared
to enter at such a time. Five boats were upset,
most very near it, and one brig with stores,
aground, as well as one small ship of war, a gun-
vessel, I believe, and some never got in at all.
The place fixed for the bridge was not so wide as
was expected and prepared for, so sufficient boats
are ready, and last night all but about three were
moored in their berths ready, and I should think
the bridge would to-day be passable.

The loss of the French in the gun-boats and
corvettes was greater than we supposed, for the
inhabitants inform us, a Captain of cannoniers
was killed, and several men, and the Captain of the
corvette lost his arm. The rockets also did mischief on shore, one man who is now in here, had

both legs carried off by a rocket. I have been since told, the French lay down on their faces, and then ran away from them. An order has been issued in Bayonne for all persons who have not and cannot procure six months' provisions to quit the town, and numbers were coming this way along the road yesterday. I went out that way on purpose to meet them, and talk to them. They all agreed in the number of men, about eleven thousands, but said a great part were conscripts and weakly.

This I concluded of course, as all those unequal to an active campaign would be naturally left in the walls for quiet garrison duty. The alarm had been terrible in the town, which was expecting an attack two days since. Every householder was ordered to have an immense tub filled with water, ready at his door, &c. Count Reille was gone to the rear, some said ill, and Thouvenot commanded again, and most said Marshal Soult was gone to Paris, some to Mount Marsan, and Count Gazan commanded. A Frenchman, who came yesterday, told Monsieur d'Arcangues, an inhabitant here, that he had just passed through La Vendée, and that country, and that it was in arms again; that he had himself seen several armed parties; amounting some of them to seven or eight hundred men. This will at the least stop the conscription a little.

I communicated this good news to *son Altesse Royale,* and at the same time made him a little *cadeau,* by begging he would let me send him King Joseph's saddle cloth, which I had picked up at Vittoria, but had never used, as being rather too splendid, (blue with a very broad gold border). He was very civil, and in return lent me a paper of the 11th, which he had just got out with his baggage from England, a second edition of the *Courier,* containing in the corner a notice of the arrival of the message through France from Lord Castlereagh, a piece of news which alarmed him not a little, though our French accounts still say the negociations are broken off, and the Allies close to Paris.

General Harispe had raised about three thousand or three thousand eight hundred of his countrymen, the Basques, a fine race of people; but since our late move, most of them have run home, and his corps, as the maire here told me yesterday, is reduced to about five hundred. Our officers remain delighted with their reception on the right; they all say that every one talks with horror of making war in an enemy's country; but that all they can say from experience is, that they never wish again to make war in a friendly one if this is to be the manner of making war in an enemy's. Nothing, I believe, has been done on the right of any consequence yet, only preparations in case this bridge failed, I believe; if so, I think we should now have Lord Wellington back here directly from Garris, where he has been, and the move will at last take place.

I have just got my mules back from Passages, with six days' hay, and am now ready, though my Guardsman tailor has carried half my new clothes with him across the Adour, and I never expect to see them more, and have a Frenchman at work with some new jobs. Considering your lost box and all contingencies, I think my last suit will stand me in about 35*l.* sterling!

The ride along the high road to Bayonne, was yesterday an interesting scene. The refugees from the town, several of them very pretty Basques, were all coming this way, laden with the little baggage they could carry off. Our artillery all moving up the contrary way; as well as the Spanish troops; and

hundreds of Basques, men and women, with great
loads on their heads (like our Welch fruit-women
going to Covent-garden), only their baskets were
full of bread, biscuits, &c., and all in requisition for
the Spaniards. The bât animals and baggage parties of the Spaniards, are not a little amusing, and
their led chargers with their tails buckled up, and in
swaddling clothes, with dirty magnificent housings,
&c., and dancing about half-starved, with their
heads in the air. Every fifty yards a dead bullock
or horse, but chiefly the former, and every two
hundred, an ox dying, and a Spanish muleteer or
straggler waiting until the bullock driver abandoned him, to turn him up, and cut his heart out,
before he was dead, but when in a state too weak
to resist. The heart alone seemed to be worth the
trouble, as nothing else could be cut off from the
bones, and bone and all did not pay the cutting up
and carriage.

The destruction and present price of cattle are
tremendous, and I grieve to hear we have been
obliged to give the Spaniards a lot of our best
Irish cattle, as we had no other at hand. The
only meat they seemed to have with them, was a
number of ox cars with sides of Spanish bacon;

this, and sardines seemed to form their supply. The men, however, I still say, are very fine men, and I am sure well commanded would make excellent troops. Nevertheless, I was by no means sorry to find we had still an English brigade of about twelve or fifteen hundred men (Lord Aylmer's) between us and the eleven thousand French at Bayonne, as I am sure five thousand French would force their way through the fifteen thousand Spaniards if they chose to try, though we should in the end prevent their return. At any rate we should have early notice, and alarm from the runaways. The French beat our fellows at that, as we cannot catch them, and the Spaniards would not be easily caught by the French.

We had a most anxious scene here two nights since. Just as our vessels got into the Adour, a suttling brig, Dutch-built, and very strong, to save pilotage fees, tried to get in (without the pilot boats) to this river. The boats towing missed the mouth, were both swamped, and the men in most imminent danger, as well as the vessel, which was driven in without guidance, aground for an hour, but saved, and at last all lives saved, or at least all but one. When the boat was filled, another wave drove it against the ship, and three caught hold of the ship chains and got in; the fourth was knocked about in the water between the ship, the boat, and the wall, but at last got his chin on the sinking boat, came up the harbour so, was hailed in and saved. In my morning walk on the sea wall, I found another ship on shore, a large brig with a valuable cargo, a private speculation. This will be the third wreck, but considering how many vessels have been here, and how they have been all exposed, and half of them absolutely at the mercy of any north or north-west squalls, we have, I think, been most fortunate.

Later.—In my ride to-day I met about thirty or forty wounded men of the Buffs and 39th second division; but this is the consequence of the last move, I believe, as they told me they were wounded at or near Cambo. We have reports of an affair, but here know nothing as yet. We are becoming, instead of being like head-quarters, the centre of all good information, a mere hospital station in the rear, and famous, as usual, for ill-founded reports, which the medical men, I suppose, invent from *ennui* on these occasions. A large brig has arrived from Bordeaux with wine, but, I should think, almost too late for the speculation.

Sunday, 27th February, Post-day.—In my walk

this morning I saw another boat swamped, trying to get out of the river over the bar. It was actually worked by the surf into this position, with the stern stuck into the sand of the bar, and fairly went over, with the five men. For some time all five were visible, two swimming, and three clinging to the keel of the wreck, which was bottom uppermost. Another boat, which had intended to follow this one out, was fortunately close at hand, just out of the reach of the surf, and by this means the two swimmers were saved by giving them a rope's end, and also one of the three from the wreck, as it floated inwards. There was a struggle between the three, when a wave came, and two appeared no more. The relations of the two men witnessed their loss, as well as myself, standing on the edge of the wall within ten yards of the men, but unable to help them. The distress you may conceive. We become in some degree hardened by seeing death so continually, and in so many forms, as we do here.

I have also this morning met with five English seamen, part of the crew of one of our provision ships, which were lost some months since on this coast. The master and four men, being from St.

Andars, and the French having heard of the fever there at that time, they were put under quarantine on the coast, about forty miles on the other side of Bayonne. Afterwards they escaped, and lived about among the inhabitants, who, they say, treated them well, as the master had money. At last, hearing from the French that we had crossed the Adour, they made through the woods this way, and fell in with our cavalry about three leagues the other side of Bayonne, General Vandeleur being on that side of the Adour, with two regiments. They mention that they saw on the road going to Dax a number of the wounded French from Bayonne, and also troops retiring that way, the people told them, to the amount of fifteen thousand, but the number must have been exaggerated, I think, and that considerably.

The servant of Captain Pitts, of the Engineers, came in yesterday with an account of his master's death. Captain Pitts was one of General Cole's staff, and a most spirited, zealous, skilful, and promising young man. He was killed on the right a few days since, when our men had driven the French over the Gave d'Oleron. He went down to reconnoitre, and take a sketch of the banks, and make observations with a view to a bridge. His servant says he had finished, and was looking round just before he came off, when a ball struck him on the head. General Cole's staff have been very unfortunate this last year, and indeed the loss of officers in his whole division has been very considerable. I used to think that it sometimes affected his spirits, though it never induced him to endeavour to diminish it, as he always was and would be foremost in danger.

Count Damas has just informed me, that Lord Wellington has now crossed both the Gaves, and is near Orthes; but we have no authentic news from him.

All accounts agree that General Picton was wounded in the affair on crossing the Gave; but, it is said, not badly.

I picked up this morning a Spanish paper, and, on making it out, found it was a letter from a Spanish officer in camp, near Bayonne, telling some friend in the rear that Murillo and Mina had beat the French across the Gave, and were in pursuit along with two English divisions, having taken forty guns, &c., and then saying the inhabitants were *muy malos*, but that we treated them as well as Spaniards, and that they, the Spaniards, were ordered to do the same, but that we should see, &c.

Head-Quarters, St. Jean de Luz, February 28, 1814.—Lieut.-Colonel C—— is now returned here, and we have at length some authentic accounts of what has passed. Lord Wellington was at Orthes, where he left him, intending to stay there a short time to arrange communications with General Hope's column, &c. Our men forded the Gave de Pau, and drove the enemy from Orthes. As they made some stand in that town, it was a little *rompé'd,* as we call it. General Picton was not wounded, and our loss has been inconsiderable upon the whole. Colonel C—— returned by my old road through Peyrehorade, Ramons, and across the Adour, at Port de Lanne, and so to Bayonne, and then across the new bridge here. He found the first division driving the French from the heights above the citadel of Bayonne, close into the town last night. This was done, but with some loss and much firing. Those hills are important, as in some measure commanding the citadel. To-morrow we march to join head-quarters. I believe we shall not pass the new bridge, as a Spanish army crosses that way, and will occupy it all day, and the road also. In addition to which, we have, as yet, only cavalry patroles along the road, and the French have halted a force at Dax, or Acks, or Ax (in the different maps). I understand we are to go by Ustaritz, Hasparran, Garris, Sauveterre, and Orthes. This is a roundabout bad road, but will, to me, be a new country. Our weather, most luckily, continues fine as yet.

Our accounts from the interior are, that Toulouse and Bordeaux are both ready to hoist the white flag, and only wait for our sanction and declaration. This point of etiquette may spoil all. I think we should declare our readiness to support them the moment they declare publicly their readiness to take that part. It is a critical moment. Many are alarmed at Schwartzenburg's not having made more progress; he seems to have hung back, as his army was stronger than Blucher's, and was forwarded six weeks since, and yet we only hear of Blucher near Paris. I must now prepare to "*romper de march*," as Jack Portugoose calls it. So adieu.

CHAPTER II.

PASSAGE OF THE RIVER — START FOR ORTHES — EFFECT OF
THE BATTLE — FEELINGS OF THE FRENCH — WELLINGTON
WOUNDED—ST. SEVER — CHURCH AND SCHOOL — AIRE —
WELLINGTON ON THE CONDUCT OF THE ALLIES — INDU-
RATING EFFECTS OF WAR.

Head-Quarters, St. Sever,
March 5th, 1814.

MY DEAR M——

HERE I am again with head-quarters, and
within two leagues of my old quarter, Mont de
Marsan. We have had a most unpleasant, and for
the baggage animals, a most laborious journey,
from the terrible state of the weather—hail-storms,
rain storms, with violent south-westerly winds almost all the time. By warm clothing and good
living I have escaped with only one day's return of
rheumatism, which has now gone off, and I feel in
very tolerable repair.

On the 1st of March we left St. Jean de Luz,

and passed the grand bridge below Bayonne, in sight of, and I really believe within gun-shot of the walls. We all filed over in safety, and then along the sea-wall for half a mile, with water on both sides, to Boucaut. I was surprised that the animals were not more alarmed.

The bridge answered perfectly; it consisted of thirty-six two-masted vessels, with anchors across all the way at the head and stern of each; a strong beam across the centre of each, between the masts, to which the cables were fastened, to form the road, so that each formed a separate bridge, and the destruction of one cable only affected one space. The boards were then fixed on these cables, and were interlaced all the way by small cords, through notches in the boards, and thus we went safely along between the masts, in a road about twelve or fourteen feet wide, differing, however, from a common bridge, for the arches between the boats, from the stretching of the cables, formed concaves instead of convex arches, some of them descending nearly to the water's edge. It answered, however, perfectly, and will continue to do so, unless the Spaniards suffer the French to come and destroy it. Of this I have my doubts. The crews were living in their vessels at the head and stern, cooking away and going on as usual. Five or six gun-boats were moored about it, then came the boom and boats ready to tow ashore any fire-ship.

At Boucaut we found Sir John Hope and his staff, so we were ordered to the next village on the road. Our managing Quarter-Master clumsily went to a bad village of a dozen houses, out of the road, when there was a very good one on the right road, only a few miles further. Several of us had no houses, and were told we must find them for ourselves. After waiting some time until my baggage came, I determined to go on the right road until I found a quarter vacant, trusting with full confidence to the good disposition of the inhabitants, which towards the English is most excellent. After looking into five, 1 found a vacant one a mile and a half off, no officer within half a mile, and no English troops within two miles, and none at all towards the interior of France on that road. The people expected some one, and a bed was ready and a complete welcome I received.

In my way I went round by the picket, within about eight hundred yards of Bayonne citadel, where my tailor was on fatigue duty in the works, and I thus recovered my pantaloons and waistcoat. I was just going to bed at eight o'clock, when a violent cannonading and sharp musketry commenced, sounding close by us. I did not think it prudent to go to bed until it ceased, as we were within about a mile and a half of a garrison of eleven thousand men; but suspecting what was the case, that it was only our people driving the French out of a field-work on the hill, and hemming them in closer to the citadel, I was scarcely at all alarmed.

My host and his family were great royalists in their professions, as they had for the last six months been more than usually oppressed by the French. He had a house and ten acres of land; the house worth about 10*l*. a-year in England, as I should think. His rent of the land was one-half the produce of corn and maize; the taxes on his house had been already that year sixty francs, and his contributions fifteen bushels of maize and I think ten of corn. He said no one could live if this went on, and all the young men were carried off. He had one quarter to pay still, but expecting us every day, he put it off from time to time, though much threatened, and now thought himself safe.

From thence we started early for Peyrehorade, a largish place, nearly as large as Kingston-upon-Thames. It was market-day, and the people of the country on business crowded in as usual. They all stared at us, most saluted us; all were civil, and we got our quarters with much more facility, and met with ten times the civility we had ever done in Spain. I never witnessed a single quarrel, though the town was crowded as it is at an election time with you, and we had only about twenty dragoons to protect all the one thousand two hundred animals and baggage of head-quarters.

My host was peculiarly civil, and gave me a very good apartment and an excellent dinner—some roast beef *à l'Anglaise* all red with gravy, a duck, and a fowl. The whole family dined with us, wife, mother, and two daughters. The eldest son, who had been intended for an attorney, had been taken as a conscript, and was wounded at Leipsic—since that time they had not heard of him; I comforted them by suggesting that he must have been left at Mayence. The next son was sixteen, and at school at St. Sever; next year it became his turn to take

his chance as a conscript. And you may well conceive that we were considered as welcome guests—
independently of the expectation of having coffee
and sugar cheap for grandmamma, and English
linens, muslins, &c., for the two ugly misses.

On the 3rd of March we started again for Orthes,
the scene of the famous battle, which you will have
heard before you receive this letter, and of which
we received several imperfect accounts as we went
along. The reception all along the road, and at
Orthes, was the same as at Peyrehorade; Dr.
M—— and Major G—— just stopped in the stable
of a château for shelter, and the owner came out
and took them in, gave them cold turkey and
champagne. At Orthes I got an excellent quarter
at the *Juge de Paix's*, who was very hospitable as
usual, and as the weather was so excessively bad,
and my Portuguese almost dead with their walk of
twenty miles in the rain and mud, I stopped the
night there, notwithstanding the head-quarters were
regularly eight miles further at Sault. I knew the
latter was a miserable place, and this was another
inducement.

At Orthes I found about two thousand wounded,
one thousand English, and the others French and

Portuguese ; the latter had behaved well, as
usual. I found the Adjutant-general, Pakenham,
confined to his bed, ill at the inn, but, at nine at
night and this morning, very much better. The
hospitals all established and in full activity. Lord
March was shot in the chest, but the surgeon hoped
he would do well, and thought so; he could not,
however, find the ball, but had reason to think it
had not passed the lungs. Colonel Brook's brother
(a schoolfellow of George's) was shot through the
lungs, and there is little hope of him.

The affair at Orthes was quite unexpected; as
they had suffered our army to pass all the rivers,
no one expected this desperate stand, for such I
am told it was, the French having seldom fought
better. They stood some time, even when they had
ceased to fire, and it is therefore concluded had no
ammunition left; and after our cavalry (who behaved well) was in the midst of them cutting away.
At last they gave way, and then fled quickly.
Their loss no one knows, as the wounded got off to
the villages round, but all say their army is actually
reduced above eight thousand men, as the conscripts are all running home as fast as they can;
above twenty had come back to Peyrehorade, and

one gentleman-like young man, I met at my quarter there, was a convalescent conscript, and such he said he should now always remain, unless affairs took another turn again.

Our state here is most curious; all riding about singly, entering every house we please, well received everywhere, and baggage straggling all over the country; every one saying one man had caused all their misery for the last three years. The Bourbons are almost forgotten, and few, even of the better sort of people, know who the Duc d'Angoulême is. All want peace, and therefore wished him well. The French people are just now humbled to a most astonishing degree. I could scarcely have believed it possible.

I went everywhere talking to the people, and explaining a little who our "royal tiger" is, and why he came as he did. At Flagenan I found the maire and townspeople waiting to pay their respects to him in form. This was bolder than at most places, and I was sorry to mortify them, by telling them he had already passed. At Peyrehorade, when the French army went by, every place was shut up; when we came, every place and all the shops were opened.

The horror of the Spaniards is, however, very great. Still the people would take no active part; they remained quiet, hoping for peace. At Orthes, Marshal Soult ordered the inhabitants to arm and assist, and the action was so close on a formidable position on the hills above the town, that several balls fell into the houses; instead of doing so, they all shut themselves up, and there waited the event. He vowed vengeance, and that the town should be pillaged in consequence. Of course they wished us success, as you may well conceive. In many places the French have done much injury to the inhabitants as they went off, burning mills, bridges, forage, and the suburbs of Navarens, on military accounts, but plundering also, very considerably, on private accounts. The people now fear we are too weak, and begin to tremble.

It is a trying time for them. The schoolmaster here has rubbed out his *Collège Impériale.* This may be his ruin if matters change again. At Mont de Marsan we have found immense stores, as I expected. This place, St. Sever, is larger than Orthes, or Peyrehorade, and is said to have had much *émigrée* and *ancienne noblesse.* The reception, however, as to quarters, &c., has not been quite so good as hitherto, more from alarm, I believe, than anything else.

It was curious that Lord Wellington and General Alava were close together when struck, and both on the hip, but on different sides, and neither seriously injured, as the surgeon told me who dressed them. Lord Wellington's was a bad bruise, and skin was broken: I fear his riding so much since has rather made it of more consequence, but hope the two day's halt here will put him in the right way again, as all our prospects here would vanish with that man.

From this vicinity the French took the Toulouse road, and, as you will see, made another stand near Aire. The Portuguese, I am sorry to say, ran at that place, and we were at first repulsed, but General Barnes's brigade came up, and set all to rights, by driving the French on again, and taking some prisoners. Our way here has been in some degree difficult and dangerous, from the flooded rivers and broken down bridges which, as yet, are only slightly repaired, so as to be just passable. At the Adour, we have here actually been delayed two days, I understand. At Port de Lanne, we passed it on two large rafts, and two ferry-boats, with some risk; my boat was nearly over, from two spirited horses on board, and my little mule, with his panniers on, jumped into the water. This put my linen and sugar, &c., in a pretty mess, as you may suppose, and drowned the live fowls on his back. At Peyrehorade I also lost a mule, and had to overload the rest in consequence.

At this place I last night recovered my mule, and lost nothing on the road, except the drowned fowls, which can now be replaced here. The history of all the mishaps on a march is curious. I dined at the ferry-house, and did not go away till I saw all my own nine animals clear over. Some persons have never heard of their baggage since, and are now here without it: it will turn up soon, no doubt, at least in great part.

My old host at Mont de Marsan has sent to inquire after me. One feels now quite strange in an enemy's country, meeting deserters around on the road, gens-d'armes, the same conscripts going home, and a stout peasantry with great Irish bludgeons, all very civil and friendly; and Lord Wellington, by proclamation, ordering the maires to form an armed police, and protect their own districts themselves from stragglers, muleteers, &c.

I always expected that Soult would retire towards Toulouse, to fall back on Suchet, and either hang on our flank, if we go on to Bordeaux, or draw us from the sea and our supplies if we follow him up. I think we can push on to Bordeaux and the river, and then sweep on before us towards Toulouse. Time will show Lord Wellington's plans, which no one can do more than guess at. In the end I was right as to his crossing the Gaves in force.

I have just met with the Baron de Barthe. He tells me all prospers with the royal cause, and that the French provinces of Poitou, Guienne, Brittany, &c., are all in open insurrection, and the white flag flying. P——'s account of the state of France on his side coincides, as you must observe, almost precisely with mine, as far as I have yet seen. The people are all at market here to-day, just as if nothing were the matter, and we were not here. As yet there is only hatred in many of the lower classes, and a few of the higher, to Bonaparte; but no effort for the Bourbons, and much alarm in the purchasers of national property. The *ancienne noblesse* is beginning to talk and to stir a little, and the *nouveaux riches* are by some laughed at. Public opinion begins to dare to vent itself, and the minds of the people at large are, I think, veering fast. Many think us too weak at present. It is said we move to-morrow to Aire, on the Toulouse road, but nothing is fixed. I went to inquire after Lord Wellington to-day; he was busy writing, and said he was better, and looked well enough. The Duc d'Angoulême has sent to Mont de Marsan as his agent, a *professeur*, who was despised there, and this has given offence. The truth is, that he does not know where as yet to find men of weight and talent.

St. Sever, March 6th, 1814.—The mail, I understand, is to be despatched to-day, so I add a few lines, as we halt here again to-day, and I believe to-morrow, from the flooded state of the river and the enemy having destroyed the bridges in their retreat to Auch, where we are told they now are. Marshal Soult, it is said, finding the Italians also now beginning to desert since Murat's new alliances, has ordered all Italian soldiers to be disarmed. Another story about, but not so much to be relied on, is, that Bonaparte has been badly wounded, and desired General Macdonald to put him out of his misery, and that the latter took him at his word, and shot him.

The Duc d'Angoulême was at high mass again to-day, at which some hundreds of the new levy attended, as my host tells me, known by their short cropped heads. We are here so different from what we were in Spain, that it is quite droll. I have a general invitation from my host whilst I stay. To-day I go to Lord Wellington's.

Later on the 7th.—We stay to-day, as the bridges are not repaired, and the floods have not quite subsided. I walked down to the bridge with Lord Wellington yesterday, and found him limp a little, and he said he was in rather more pain than usual, but it was nothing. At dinner yesterday, he said he was laughing at General Alava having had a knock, and telling him it was all nonsense, and that he was not hurt, when he received this blow, and a worse one, in the same place himself. Alava said it was to punish him for laughing at him. At dinner we had the new Swedish tiger, the Prince's aide-de-camp, who has been here a few days, covered with gold. His pantaloons are most *magnifique.* He seemed a good-tempered man, but I did not think very much of him.

Two of the Bordeaux people were also there, who are to return to-day, and General Frere's aide-de-camp from Peyrehorade, as he is marching up that way by Orthes. The people in office at Pau sent to say they were ready to declare for the King, and Count Damas boldly enough went over there to see the state of things. He has come back safe, and reports them ready, but that they cannot take any public step until we are in force there. Amongst other opinions and feelings here, we, the English, have our partisans. Many say they should like an English government, and Lord Wellington told me, laughing, he believed we had almost as many friends and partisans as the Bourbons. Peace certainly is by far the most popular project of all. I am excessively hurried with business to-day, and must prepare to see Lord Wellington.

Head-Quarters, Aire, March 11, 1814.—By a sudden order we moved from St. Sever to this place yesterday, so far on our road to Toulouse, and the scene of the affair a few days since, when

the Algarve brigade (all Portuguese) took to their
heels, and the English brigade of General Barnes
behaved so well.

We are now playing a bolder game than usual.
The French, as I suspected, went the Toulouse
road from St. Sever, and have a column in our
front on the road to Auch, I believe, and another
near or towards Tarbes. This leaves Bordeaux
open. To take advantage of this, we have also
divided two divisions under Marshal Beresford;
the seventh and the fourth are gone to Bordeaux, and must be by this time close to the
town, which is said to be ripe to join us, and
declare for the King. The Duc d'Angoulême is
gone that way.

In front here we have Sir Rowland Hill's corps,
the second and sixth divisions, and also the third
and light divisions; and General Frere's Spanish
army of twelve thousand men, to be fed by us, is
on its road up, to be, I understand, at St. Sever
to-day; and to support this main movement
against Soult, who is said to be near Auch. In
the meantime, General Hope remains with the
first division, including all the Guards and German
Legion (and, of course, the choice men, and in high

order, and undiminished by service nearly), and
also with the fifth division and General Don Carlos
d'Espagne's Spanish brigade, and, I believe, also
Lord Aylmer's British one, to blockade and take
Bayonne. It is most unfortunate that so large a
force should be required for that object; but we
dare not trust, I conclude, the bridge and our
communications to the Spaniard's keeping.

Great preparations are making against Bayonne,
and the garrison have been driven in very close to
the citadel; but no steps have been as yet taken
for the actual siege by regular approaches or
batteries. Our army is thus very much divided
just now, and the communications would be difficult, except that the country is with us. All the
French posting establishment has remained, and
everything nearly goes on as usual. The people
quietly let us take our own measures, and give no
opposition, though not openly declaring or helping
us. It is remarkable that we go about as if in
England, and yet no mischief has been done either
to officers, men, or baggage. If the country
people had been like the Spaniards and against
us, what we are now doing would have been out
of the question. Half our army, by straggling

about, would have been knocked on the head.   We have, fortunately, just now plenty of money, and pay for everything; and the English are in the highest repute.

In general, also, we have behaved well.   There are, however, many instances to the contrary; and many more, I am sorry to say, amongst the Portuguese.   When the Spaniards come, I am much afraid things will be much worse.   The mischief done by, and injury arising from, the passing of the very best disciplined army is considerable. The people feel that, and are ready, in general, to submit to much, especially as the French army has been so much worse than ours, and does not pay for anything, whilst, on the other hand, we enable many to make almost little fortunes against quiet times; and Lord Wellington begins upon a plan, which I only hope he will have funds to continue, of paying for all damage done when well made out. Indeed, some most exaggerated and unreasonable demands have been made to him in consequence. Guineas are already spread all over this province, and pass most readily.

I am at an apothecary's here, who was, I am sorry to say, robbed by our men just after the attack. General Hill offered to send him the money, nearly 15*l.* and a watch; but he declined taking it.

Lord Wellington has a cold, but rode here yesterday in his white cloak, in a terribly cold day, with the snow right in his face; for we have now got another little winter here, which is unusual. I have had some fever and cold, but am better again; indeed, much as usual, after a little discipline at St. Sever.

At the latter place, there was a large church built by the English. In general, it is exactly in the style we call Saxon or old English, circular arches and Saxon ornaments. I suspect, however, it must have been built just as the Gothic style was beginning to come into fashion, as the side aisle arches and part of the body of the church were pointed or Gothic; and this did not appear to have been, like some of ours, a subsequent alteration. A handsome small old Corinthian façade was inserted within the large Saxon heavy arch which formed the original entrance of the front of the church. In the town was a very good school, called *Le Collège Impériale.* About ninety-two boys were then in the school, who all re-

mained, and were very civil to our officers whenever we went there. The boys seemed to wish us
well, I thought; and they do not usually conceal
their real opinions. The establishment was in an
old Benedictine abbey, and was exceedingly good.
The lower cloisters and the great church, gutted
at the Revolution, formed excellent play-places; and
the great corridors above were all half enclosed by
small wooden rooms for the boys, each having one
to himself, about eight feet by five, holding his bed,
his chair, table, and box; and, by being all open
at the top to the gallery, they were airy and yet
retired and private. The expense of this school is
about 400 francs, or 20l. a-year. For this, Latin,
writing, French, geography, music, dancing, and a
little mathematics were taught. Some boys could
read Livy, Tacitus, and Cicero. The dinners and
other arrangements, are cleanly and good. Napoleon gave them the building. The funds were
all private, no foundation, lands, or allowances from
Government.

The road from St. Sever here was through a
rich flat bottom near the Adour, with a high bank
all the way on the south side, with several
chateaux. We crossed the Adour to come here at

Sever, over our newly-made bridge; came along
the great road on the north bank, and re-crossed
again at a ferry at this place, this for the fourth
time since we left St. Jean de Luz. The country
seems well cultivated, and in appearance not unlike parts of the Bath road, in Berkshire—a flat
corn country, with wooded, rising grounds and villas
at some distance, which formed the valley. We
passed Grenade, a largish village about eight miles
from St. Sever, and a large chateau at about six
miles off, belonging to the Marquis de St. Maurice,
the chateau taking his name. We also, about
four miles further on, passed a small village, called
Cageres; and four miles more brought us here.
The bridge at Barcelonne is about a mile and a
half high up, over the Adour, and has not been
destroyed by the French; they only broke one
arch of wood, which we have repaired: we were to
have crossed there to get hither, but I came almost
the first, found a ferry just re-established, and came
over; most followed the same way.

Aire is not so large a town as St. Sever or
Orthes,—it is about the size of Epsom. It
is close to the river, is old and dirty, and half
deserted. Several good houses gutted, or at least,

without furniture; and the ruins of a very large modern-built bishop's palace, destroyed during the Revolution, when, I believe, this place suffered much. At Upper Aire, which stands well on a hill half a mile above this, is a celebrated school or college, or rather two united. It was first formed about sixty or eighty years since, a handsome building erected for the purpose, and well contrived, in plan much like that at St. Sever. It was in great repute before the Revolution, but was then destroyed, and almost completely gutted. Within the last ten years, the professors and clergy have, by degrees, by charities, charity sermons, and great exertions, nearly restored the whole again without government assistance; and, before this late attack, there were above two hundred boys there. In one building there are above a hundred boys, all destined for the church; in another, above a hundred for lay employments. An old church built by the English, but much altered, and in a much later style than that at St. Sever, stands between the schools, is for their use as a church, and unites the two establishments; the whole having a good broad play terrace on the brow of the hill above the river.

Education is here cheaper than at St. Sever, though there are no government funds at either. The yearly cost is about three hundred or three hundred and fifty francs. I rather think clothing was, however, included in the estimate at St. Sever, and that would make the two much alike. The studies are the same. It put me in mind of Maynooth College, near Dublin, and seemed what our colleges were three or four centuries ago.

My patron or host at St. Sever, was a sort of small landholder and noble, with his house in town and villa two miles off, which dated, as he took care to tell me, 130 years, as the builder's mark and his ancestor's name proved, and therefore, " *C'est clair, mais ce n'est rien pour moi, c'est bien vrai maintenant que ma famille est supérieure à celle de M. le Maire de notre ville,*" &c. M. le Maire had made most of his money by dabbling with national property during the revolution, and succeeded better than many others here; " but," continued my host, " as I have always been considered one of the noblesse, I have suffered accordingly, *mais n'importe,* I am grown a philosopher. I never can see such times as Robespierre's again; so I see English, Spanish, Portuguese, and all with indifference, and remain quiet. At the same time I am now English (he always said *nous autres*, which often puzzled me) and I wish the cause well, and would contribute much to its success." He seemed surprised that his contribution of maize for our horses was all paid for instantly, and that in gold, and at a fair good price, even though M. le Maire who managed it (no one knew for what) detained eleven sous out of every eighty from all to whom he made payments. M. La Borde de Menos was my host's name, he was very civil, and I dined with his family, his wife, two daughters, and a son, whenever I was not engaged, which happened only twice, at Lord Wellington's. He also gave my men wine, &c.; in short, I believe he rejoiced much at the change he had experienced in having me instead of a whole company of officers, men and all, which he had one day when we first came.

In return for his treatment I bought toys for the lad; gave some tea to Madame in case of sickness, and a pretty cadeau to Mademoiselle. In a word we parted excellent friends. The many stories he told me of what had passed in Robespierre's time were curious. M. La Borde was obliged to act with the Representant, and attend all meetings, to be only pillaged and abused by every one, and to bow and say, "Thank you all," with his hat in his hand; and this was to prevent their having an excuse for guillotining him, as thirty of the principal people were put to death in the small town of St. Sever. The living alone and staying away was of itself a heinous offence, and every requisition of a cart for a day's use was called for *sous peine de mort.* That was the form of all demands. A ball was given by the Representant. Every one must go or be suspected. Madame went. She had a valuable gold watch-chain; but not daring to show it, she went with a cut steel one. The Representant said, "*Mais où est donc votre chaine d'or? Le publique en a besoin.*" She was obliged to swear it had been stolen, and to hide it ever afterwards. The Representant seemed incredulous, and the risk of this fraud was great, but it answered. Monsieur was not so lucky; he had a valuable ring, he attended one of the meetings with it on. The Representant said, "*Tu F—— Noble. donnez moi ta bague, ce n'est par pour des gens comme toi; le publique en a besoin.*" He took it off and gave it up, and some months after saw it on the finger of one of the Representant's relations.

I have now a will to draw up in case of accident, for Sir N. P——, Bart., to secure 10,000*l*. to each of his younger children.   He is here with his regiment; so adieu.

Lord Wellington abuses the Allies for having been beaten, when they had the game in their hands; and says, one ran his head against the Marne, and the other against the Seine, and the whole was ill-managed.

We have the further news of a French column having made its way from Lyons to near Geneva again; but a report still later, that the Allies have, under Blucher, got into Bonaparte's rear.   These checks are, even if they end in nothing, of the greatest use to him.   They deter people from declaring their opinions; may make every difference in that way here and at Bordeaux; and I should not be surprised if they encouraged Marshal Soult to make another stand near here, on this side the Garonne, which I do not think he would otherwise have done.

I am told he is in a position at present from Tarbes to Plaisance, on a ridge of hills, and that the country is full of positions.   My news is from M. D——, the husband of my young Spanish

Bilboa lady, who came to me to-day. They have left Bayonne from fear, and are waiting the events of the war at Pau, whence he came over here,— and like a true placeman, thinking matters were about to change, he insinuated to me that he should like an appointment under the new order of things—under the direction of the Bourbons or the English.

He also wanted a passport for his little wife's brother to go back to Bilboa, from General Alava. I have got him that; but on condition that the civil authorities are written to, and the brother examined on his arrival, as to his conduct, &c. M. D—— was Colonel F——'s friend and not mine; and I own I had no great opinion of him, but thought he was only attentive to Colonel F—— to serve his own purposes, and seemed to be rather an intriguing gentleman. It is, however, quite my principle that every one should be allowed to go home, and go about his business; and I am sure that Spain will profit by the residence of any one who has lived at all with the French, and acquired some notions of what mankind are capable of, and of human exertion.

In my walks to-day, I met a poor gentleman who told me we had taken all his forage, and that his oxen were starving, and that he must sell them; he was going to a contractor for that purpose. I advised him to go to our Commissary Haines, and took him, and introduced him, as I thought each would gain by a bargain direct. His oxen are to be inspected to-morrow. During our conversation, he told me he was the brother-in-law of Dulau, the French bookseller in Soho Square, and that the latter had no nearer relation, but that he could never hear of him, or write to him. I undertook to send his letter. If such a letter is enclosed to you, therefore, you will know all about it, and my poor man may get a legacy or something by it, from the great Mr. Dulau, for such he must be.

Saturday, March 12th.—We remain here to day, and I think shall do so for a few days, unless the French move off. We seem to be moving up. A brigade of artillery and some troops were yesterday taking the direction of Pau, to secure that town, I conclude, as we have now only artillery there, and also, perhaps, to turn the left of the French position at Tarbes. Lord Wellington is better; his hounds go out to-day, and I should not be surprised at his being out with them. As a proof how savage war makes everyone, even an English soldier, I may tell you that poor H——'s body was stript by the English soldiers of his own division, to which he was acting as Adjutant-general, and almost before his body was cold. I believe two or three fellows have been flogged for this. By degrees we all get hardened to anything.

I find the same sort of custom here as to letting and, as near Bayonne. The landlord puts a peasant into a little farm, furnishes it, pays the taxes, and finds the necessary cattle, beasts, and horses, &c., for the cultivation of the land; in return, he receives the full half of the clear produce as rent, but in kind, and very little money is seen. Before we came bread was three sous the pound, which would be about sixpence three-farthings the quartern loaf. A goose has been five francs of late, but that is dear. Fowls are now only half-a-crown or three shillings each, and very good even to the English. If we remain long in a place, we soon raise the price.

CHAPTER III.

REPORTS FROM THE SEAT OF WAR—THE DUKE D'ANGOULEME —THE GERMAN CAVALRY—MISCONDUCT OF THE SPANIARDS — ATTACKS ON OUR GRAZING PARTIES — MOVEMENT OF HEAD-QUARTERS—DEATH OF COLONEL STURGEON—VISIT TO THE HOSPITAL—NEW QUARTERS—SKIRMISHES—WELLINGTON AND THE MAYOR.

Head-Quarter Aire,
March 16, 1814.

MY DEAR M——

HERE we remain still, and I think shall do so for a few days, as the French Marshal not only keeps his position near Conchez, across our road to Tarbes and Toulouse, but does not seem to be disposed to go beyond demonstrations, and cannot muster courage to attack us, and we, I believe, are not quite prepared to attack him. The glorious reception Marshal Beresford met with at Bordeaux, and the spirited and decided conduct of the maire, &c., there, you will have heard by the last mail, as the news came after my letter, but before Lord

D 3

Wellington's bag was despatched. We have all sorts of reports from the vicinity of Paris, as to the battle at Meaux, as to a large French corps having gone over to Bernadotte. There are reports from Bordeaux, but all uncertain; I think, however, that the maire must have had some good intelligence to induce him to take the line he has done, which must be his ruin, and that of all his friends, if we make peace at last with Bonaparte.

The Duc d'Angoulême, at first, I am told, declined a burgher guard, and preferred an English one; this will not do, he must show confidence and spirit, and rely upon his French friends, and give no offence by English partialities. I think it was bad advice in some one about him, as I understand he personally has always wished to take a decided line, and risk his personal safety for the cause.

We hear the Royalist party are beginning à la lanterne again, but I hope this is not true. The inhabitants of Bordeaux must arm and protect themselves. We shall leave but a small force there. The river and their own people must be their chief reliance. Lord Wellington has sent for the fourth division from Marshal Beresford to help here.

Canning went off at four o'clock, on the 14th, with these orders (as I understand); he was sent from Gartin by Lord Wellington, eleven miles from this in front, and was here in an hour. Whilst he was dressing and getting a fresh horse, I got him his money from the Paymaster, and he was off, re-mounted, for Roquefort, twenty miles; and from thence he was to post the other seventy miles all night to Bordeaux. He was heard of at Langon, about three or four in the morning, so that by nine o'clock on the 15th, he would be in Bordeaux, and as the fourth division would march that day from Langon (where they were), in about two days more, they will be here by that time. All our eighteen-pounders and some other reinforcements will arrive, and then Soult must be off, or I hope get another beating.

The heavy German Cavalry (for by this name they wish to be known, as it carries credit with it), went through here two days since in admirable order, the horses in particular, but the latter are already too slight for the men, who are all large bony heavy men of a certain age, and all ex-perienced heroes. It will not be easy by a royal order, and light jackets and caps, to transform

these gentlemen into light Germans, nor do the
corps like it at all. Ponsonby's heavy brigade is
also close by, fresh from Spain, like the Germans,
and in the same excellent condition. Nearly ten
thousand Spaniards are also two miles from this,
at or near Barcelona, very fine-looking men, and
in good discipline. Hitherto they have also
behaved in general much better than was expected
on the march; but we feed them, as they have
no transport. If they will but fight a little in
return, and take their share of loss, we should do
famously.

Murillo's Spaniards, I am sorry to say, have
begun very ill in our front. The day before
yesterday, Soult made an advance against them,
they were ordered to fall back a little to a rivulet,
and there defend themselves. Once with their
backs turned, however, away they went, and never
stopped until the Buffs were ordered up to stop
the French, who, the moment they saw the red
coats coming on, were off home again very quickly,
but not quite so rapidly as the Spaniards had run
from them.

The Portuguese cavalry had a little affair, and
behaved well. The 14th Dragoons had also an

affair the day before yesterday. Half a squadron under Captain Babbington were ordered by Colonel Harvey to drive off a French half squadron, and then halt until he came up. They upset the French, saw another whole squadron beyond, were tempted to go on by their first success, and succeeded, in a great measure, again, but Captain Babbington was taken. The wounded French dragoons brought in here prisoners are all very fine men, of the 5th regiment, and the whole regiment are said to be the same sort of men. They came in much cut about the head and hands.

The forage animals of head-quarters were yesterday very nearly getting into a terrible scrape—about two hundred and fifty animals, and two of mine of the number. They foolishly went in front of our pickets, or nearly so, though regularly under commissariat directions. Whilst they were loading at a farm, one peasant slipt away, and it is concluded, told some French dragoons near what was going on, whilst the other in the house gave some of the party wine. There were four artillerymen, unarmed, in the house, and about six Portuguese, one of whom was mine, when a French officer of cavalry, with his sword drawn, came to the window,

told them all to come out, and that they were
prisoners. When out, seeing he was alone, and
that his party was three or four hundred yards off,
they mounted their mules, and were all off nearly,
with the loss of, I believe, only one man, and two
or three mules. Some fellows galloped all the way
here without their loads or cords, and at first spread
an alarm that all were taken. They arrived home
in the course of the day, and my Portuguese brought
home a load of good hay and two deserted ropes in
triumph. It is thought that the party should
have brought off the officer prisoner, but most are
satisfied with having got their own property back
again. He cut one of the artillerymen on the
finger, who put up his arm to save himself.

Another party of muleteers with stores from
Mont de Marsan to Bordeaux, with supplies for
the seventh division, to which they belonged, were
attacked three days since on their road, near
Roquefort, quite in our rear, and on our communications, by some French partizans, a sort of
guerillas called *La Bande*—these now, as I am
told, are employed by Soult—formerly a set of
douaniers, or smuggler catchers. Several mules
were killed and wounded, and, I believe, some

muleteers killed, and some of the money taken. I am much afraid the Spanish muleteers will begin to be alarmed at this. We have cavalry, however, on the road, and they will now be on the look out more in future.

We are now much crowded here. Three new Generals came in yesterday and to-day,—Sir Stapleton Cotton to-day, with about a hundred animals belonging to himself and his staff. I was turned out of my stable in consequence, though but a very bad one, and am now in a back kitchen turned into a stable. At Barcelona the Spaniards turned out the cavalry with much less ceremony. It is said a company, with a Captain at their head, gallantly charged Captain S——'s horses and bâtmen (General C——'s aide-de-camp), and were very successful. One little blood horse kicked about, broke loose, and made a good defence without injuring himself; but another horse not so quick in his retreat, received two slight bayonet wounds, and a slight cut with a sabre, and the Spaniards carried the day, behaving like heroes !

Our people are all moved in consequence, and I hope these *valorosos* and blood-thirsty gentlemen

will soon be allowed to contend with a more
glorious enemy, and will behave with equal spirit
when the opportunity shall arrive.

Our Swedish (Bernadotte's) aide-de-camp is, it
seems, to campaign with us; he is buying horses,
&c., and preparing for the field. He is a great
talker, and I understand, of this country. He
seems, from his conversation, to have served against
us under Massena, in Portugal, but how he is
what he is, I do not exactly understand.

Our weather is still very cold. Lord Wellington
would not even condescend to-day to go and look
at the French. He only sent Colonel Gordon to
go on to Gartin, and report.

Head-Quarters, 17th March, Aire. — About
three o'clock yesterday we learnt that the French
were off, and filed through Conchez, apparently on
the way to Tarbes. I think they will not venture
to go too near the mountains, but must make for
Toulouse. If not, our fourth division, which, it is
said, will be here to-night, will make us strong
enough, I hope, to push a column through Auch
straight to Toulouse, while the rest follow Soult,
and we should then be at Toulouse first. I conclude he will turn that way from Tarbes. General

Hill moved a little after the French yesterday to keep them in sight. The rest of the army will, I think, get in motion to-day or to-morrow, and head-quarters move on very soon afterwards. About fifty prisoners were sent in here last night, mostly dragoons.

We are all alive again as to the Allies, and the stories from Bordeaux are most animating. In addition to this, we move after Soult to-morrow. Head-quarters to be at Viella, three leagues in advance, nearly, towards Auch. I fear we shall, as part of head-quarters, see neither Toulouse nor Bordeaux; for if my generalship corresponds with Lord Wellington's, I think Soult will cross the Garonne, and that our right will go by Toulouse, and that we, as part of head-quarters, shall pass the river by some bridge to be laid down below near Agen,—more towards the centre of our movements. The scene at Bordeaux I much regret to have lost, and we already hear of disturbances at Toulouse, and even reports of Louis XVIII. being proclaimed at Paris. From the want of a popular Bourbon cry at Bordeaux, I hear they have set up "Henri IV." and "Gode sav de King." Our weather to-day delightful: I only hope it will last,

We are told that Suchet has offered to withdraw all his garrisons from Spain into France, and give up the towns in their present state; this has been referred, it is said, to Lord Wellington, and by him refused, as only releasing so many men for present use, who must sooner or later, if we persevere, be prisoners. This is quite right for the common cause, no doubt.

Viella, 18th.—I have just time to add a few lines at this place, which is about nine miles from Aire, on the road to Tarbes, and our head-quarters to-day. It is a small scattered village, so much so that I am at a farm at least two miles or more from the main village, and nearly by myself at the last house in the commune. I have, however, a doctor and a commissary within a quarter of a mile, and as we are fortunately well received, and welcomed everywhere, it does not signify. I feel quite at ease.

We had a tiresome march here, as the third division, the sixth, and the heavy Germans with the baggage of all the three, the whole of the pontoon train, the artillery of the two divisions, head-quarters baggage, and eight thousand Spaniards all went the same road, over our newly made bridge across the Leis, a small stream which comes into the Adour, near Barcelonne. The French in destroying this bridge, had not blown up or burnt the main centre pier, so that about twenty-five elm trees, about twenty-five feet long, and bundles of fascines, about twelve feet long, paced cross-ways, and then covered with dirt, in two days' time made us a famous bridge.

Some time hence, when the fascines get rotten, some luckless car or horseman will, I have no doubt, go through into the water, which is deep and about twenty feet below. Our high roads are excellent, and the country, though not a rich soil, very pretty and loveable. Almost every drain under the road, or a small arch for streams to pass under, had been broken down; some left so from neglect of late, some I believe just made on purpose to delay us; faggots, and a little mould, with a few small trees at bottom, soon made a passage, but created delays.

19th, 7 o'clock.—To-day we move to Mau-bourguet, nearly in the Tarbes road. This looks as if Soult was making for Tarbes, and not Tou-louse. I can scarcely believe this. If he places his rear on the mountains, he gives up Toulouse, and the richest country, and if beaten when up there, will I think escape with difficulty. He may expect some reinforcements from Suchet that way, but I think still must go to Toulouse.

We, however, have now a chance of seeing the latter, whereas I thought we should have crossed nearer Agen, lower down the river.

My patron here is very friendly. The French plundered him terribly, and all his neighbours. They call them brigands, &c., and dread them more than our army. My man let five Portuguese dragoons through his premises, and saved them, as he says. He is of a class of men that existed in former days in England; the owner and cultivator of eighty acres of land, partly corn, partly wood, partly vineyards, and partly meadow—thus he has all within himself. He has a wife and four children, two women servants, two pair of oxen, of which he has been obliged to sell one pair to pay the French contributions. He has two labourers, both deserters, for keeping whom he knows he is liable to a fine of from five hundred to three thousand francs, and to be confined five years, but he can get no other servants, and of course these are faithful.

His land, he says, is worth about 50s. an acre. It requires much labour, but when left alone he says is good enough to make them very happy. In spite of all he has suffered, and his earnest desire for peace, he is certainly no friend to the Bourbons. He curses Bonaparte for his ambition, has a tolerably just notion of all his losses in the North, and in Spain, from the soldiers, &c.; but still I think, would rather have Bonaparte still, and peace, than the Bourbons. I can never get him to say a word as to the latter, good or bad. At the same time, like all the rest of the French, he would just now submit to anything for peace. All have the highest respect for Lord Wellington, which they say they learn from the French army, high and low.

Maubourguet, 5 *o'clock.*—We left Viella at nine, and after a tiresome ride through baggage the whole way, arrived here about four, though it is only about fifteen miles. The bridges were all broken down, and every gutter nearly across the road, but this only caused delays and was quite ineffectual. The troops and artillery waggons, &c., all found some way round or through. When about twelve miles on our road we found the last

three miles quite choked with all the baggage of
head-quarters and the troops.   At first I conceived
it was a broken bridge repairing, and was patient;
but a sharp firing and cannonade soon commenced
in front of Maubourguet, near Vic, and then, guess-
ing that it was an intentional halt, I made my
way through it here, and found every one in front,
and a sharp firing about four miles in advance,
near Vic Bigorre.

I also met a party of the fine German cavalry
wounded going to the rear; they had had an affair
the day before yesterday in advance of Madiran,
half-way between that place and this, and with
two squadrons upset instantly four squadrons of
French chasseurs, took many horses, and cut up
many men, but the French ran too fast to leave
any prisoners.   This tempted the Germans to
attack yesterday a very superior force, I am told
three times their number—three French regiments
—and I hear they suffered much.

In the first affair they had about four killed and
eighteen wounded.   We were at first without orders
as to staying here and unpacking, but a report soon
came that the French would not stand and were
off; so we all unpacked quietly before the firing

ceased and prepared for dinner in this town, where five hundred French cavalry had passed the night, and had only departed with the curses of the inhabitants about eight in the morning. Our Portuguese were principally engaged, I hear, yesterday, and without much loss. The sixth division entered Vic last night.

Maubourguet, 7 o'clock, 20th, Sunday.—No orders last night. Lord Wellington very late home; but I have just learned that we move to-day to Tarbes, taking it for granted the French will be out to make room for us. This is very strange, and so is the confidence of our men. When we were halted yesterday the bâtmen were saying when within three miles of this place, the head-quarters, " We must only wait a little, till the troops have cleared our quarters for us and made room."

I now cannot understand Soult's plans. He seems to be making for the mountains, and to have suffered us in some measure to cut him off from Toulouse. Colonel Canning arrived last night from Bordeaux with an account of a grand defeat of Bonaparte's, and that he had fallen back on Orleans; this I expected, if he were not killed,

as I concluded he would try and unite with the
Lyons army and Soult's, and make one more stand
in the heart of the kingdom. If this be true, Lord
Wellington must be careful as to passing the
Garonne : Soult's junction will at any rate be
doubtful nevertheless. Our men are in the highest
spirits, and driving all before them : weather fine.

Tournay, March 21st.—At nine left Maubourguet; about four miles further I stopped at Vic
Bigorre, to see poor Colonel Sturgeon's body—a
very clever man and officer, and particularly skilful
as a bridge engineer, and in all languages, &c. He
went too close to the skirmishers, to reconnoitre,
and was shot in the head just under the eye. I
also went over the hospital, to assist Dr. M'Gregor
in giving directions to the French as to arrangements, to talk to, and satisfy some wounded French
officers, and to get from the maire bedding, straw,
and help by requisition instantly. We had about
two hundred wounded there of all nations, many
Portuguese, one of whom was undergoing the
operation of having his leg and thigh cut off, very
high up, and seemed in great agony. The French
surgeon thought Dr. M'Gregor was finding fault,
and stopped, and turned to us to explain. I un-

derstand he was doing it in a clumsy way, but Dr. M'Gregor begged I would praise him highly, or he would be alarmed, and do it still worse. Close to Vic, by the road side, were about a dozen bodies, killed by cannon-shot and terribly mauled.

Having loaded a mule with oats from a French store at Vic, I proceeded towards Tournay. The road was crammed, and some sharp skirmishing going on about three miles beyond the town, which had commenced on the Vic side. The French only left the town about nine, and tried to blow up the bridge, but were stopped by two or three gun-shots. They stood their ground tolerably, on a very strong ridge of hills, until night, and remained *en bivouac* on them last night. At three this morning they were off, and here we are after them again, about nine miles on the road to Toulouse, at this place, Tournay, which was last night Marshal Soult's head-quarters.

Tarbes is a good town, and contains a number of good houses. From the houses being large, and having yards and gardens, and from there being one or two large open spaces or squares, it covers a good deal of ground, but does not count, as I understand, above ten or eleven thousand inhabitants.

The people received us in general very well, but were quite passive, taking no part in any way. They had been kept quite in ignorance of all that was going on in the north and at Bordeaux in particular—at least a great part of them. I explained and harangued all I could to set them right. My own patron was, I suspect, a strong Bonapartist, and I took some pains to plague him a little accordingly. We have had no sort of interruption to-day, but from the multitudes passing, which form a stream, lasting from five in the morning, along a wide road, until about four or five in the day. Our fine weather is unfortunately turned to rain, but I hope will return to us again.

You will see by the map that Soult has taken to the Toulouse road at last. I hear he is at Mont St. Jean to-day, and that, as usual, when inclined to run, the French beat our people in marching, and we cannot cut him off. He has run some risks by going this round-about road, and had we been strong enough to have pushed along the Auch road also, we should have puzzled him a little; we shall now, I conclude, drive him gradually to the Garonne. I do not think he will make another stand. I have been turned out of my stable, and had much trouble with the maire, &c, so have only time to seal up, and to hope that I am not too late.

P.S. The country, from Maubourguet to Vic, Tarbes, and part of the way here, was all a flat, of rich country, like the country between Bridgewater and across into Somersetshire, except that half the meadows at least were vineyards and orchards in one, and interlaced very prettily; the fruit-trees kept small, about ten feet high, and the vines trained off at about six, and all intertwined and furled together with withy-bands. This was famous cover, as no musket-ball could pass far through the trees; a few common shot had destroyed the quincuncx regularity in many places. The water meadows were very beautiful, and the system seemed to be understood and well managed; the streams beautifully clear. The back-ground of this large flat, was, all the way to the Haute Pyrenees, covered with snow, but the higher Pic du Midi was never visible, always in the clouds; the lower one was.

The Alps are far superior, as far as I can judge. Adieu.

Nine o'clock at night, Isle en Dodon, March

24th, 1814.—Our post and movements are now so uncertain and sudden, that I know not when or how to write to you, and I fear my last was sent too late, and may probably be received with this, by which means all the zest of late news from the army will be lost. I have just heard by accident that a mail goes to-night, and have only time to scribble a few hasty lines immediately after dinner. My last finished at Tournay; from thence we proceeded the next day to Galan, a poor village and rather a wild mountain road, the short cut to Toulouse. Our second division and cavalry followed the enemy along the high road by Lannernezon, Mont St. Jean, and St. Gaudens. One corps of their army went also through Galan. The maire of the latter was a fine old man of eighty-two, and a good friend.

I was at a miserable half-furnished house, and my baggage being stopped by the Spanish troops, I did not get it until seven o'clock; but luckily got it in time to dress and get on my horse to go and dine with Lord Wellington, a mile off in the rain. The maire had been an hour in the room with Lord Wellington before he found him out, talking by the fire in his quarter, until at last

Lord Wellington having let him go on some time asked him to dinner. This staggered him and led to an explanation. The maire said that the night before he had had Generals Clausel and Harispe, and that they only ordered a dinner to be prepared, and did not ask him to eat part of his own, or thanked him, or took the least notice of him. He could not therefore believe that Lord Wellington was the enemy's General, having been so treated, as he said, "like a dog" by his friends.

My own patron was a half-starved apothecary without medicines or drugs. He offered to dress a fowl for me, but was very willing instead to sell me one for twice its value, for dinner the next day.

23rd.—We moved again to Boulognes, a longish march, about sixteen miles, and in part bad road, though in general the roads all over this part of France disgrace us in England very much; compared with our best roads, they are very superior to any in the distant counties, and to many of our main and best roads, even in the neighbourhood of London. The light, third, fourth, and sixth divisions, cavalry, and about eight thousand Spaniards, all move with this column, and we reach of course by mid-day, when all is in motion, with the artillery

and baggage, about ten miles. The second division
and cavalry follow the French. At St. Gaudens
our 13th Dragoons came up with the French rear
cavalry, formed just outside the town, charged,
broke them, drove them pell-mell through the town
on their reverse beyond it. There they re-formed;
the 13th charged again; then the French ran, with
the 13th after them, for two miles. The result is
said to be a hundred and twenty prisoners and
horses, besides killed.

From Boulognes we to-day marched to this
place—Isle en Dodon. The majority of the people
here seem to be friends of Bonaparte, and the
assistant maire in particular, with whom I had
much conversation, as he gave Doctor Hume and
me a joint billet at the empty house where he gave
out the billets, and no stable at all, and as I was
obliged to have him in the room so long, I determined to work him a little for treating us so ill.

The maire of Boulognes ran away at first. At
night he came back and went to Lord Wellington.
He showed him his proclamations and regulations,
&c. The maire said he had taken the oath to
Bonaparte, and would not act. "Very well,"
said Lord Wellington, "then the people must

choose another; but now you have taken your
line, I must take mine, and send you over the
Garonne into the French lines." He gave orders
accordingly to Colonel S——. The maire ran
away and could not be found. Colonel S——
took up the father to march him off until the son
appeared. This brought him out; he remonstrated
with Lord Wellington, said he was one of the first
men of the country, &c., and should be ruined
by this. Lord Wellington said, "He should have
thought of that sooner, and he must go," and to
this place he came to-day a prisoner.

We have just received orders to march to
Samatan to-morrow; all here have a notion that
Suchet's forces join Soult near here—that is, have
done so, or are to do so; but we are a little in the
dark, and the ignorance of the French about everything is astonishing; they seem quite stupified.
But Bonaparte has many friends still, and the
reports in the French papers, though upon the
whole good, are not decisive. The armistice seems
to have gone off from the arrangements about
Italy. We are living like the rest of the armies
and the French by requisitions; but we as yet

pay in money, which others do not; we consume everything, however, like locusts.

Lord Wellington popped between Colonel G——— and me as we were discussing the allied battles this morning, and suddenly took a part, to my great astonishment, in our conversation.

On leaving Tarbes a party of civilians went round by Bagnières to see the baths, the rooms, &c., a sort of Spa, about twelve miles round, and where no troops had been; not an Englishman there, but they were told they would be well received, and so they were indeed. The maire made them an address, the people were in crowds, so that it required force to enable them to pass. The National Guard turned out and presented arms to them; it was like Lord Wellington's entry into Zamora (as they say), such an outcry! such a display! A ball was proposed, but as there was a French garrison about six miles off and no allied troops near, the party declined staying and went off, highly pleased with their excursion. This is very odd, for on the road we go, all is stupefaction and indifference. I should have enjoyed this, but am obliged to be very prudent now after my late escape. Adieu again.

The schoolmaster, or *prêtre*, at Boulognes had written a long poem entitled "*Mon Rêve*," a prophecy nearly of all taking place, and containing much in honour of Lord Wellington. He said he had long had it concealed, and volunteered spouting it out to us to his own great satisfaction, and it really was not bad.

CHAPTER IV.

DIFFICULTIES OF THE MARCH—FAILURE OF THE BRIDGE OF
BOATS—THE GARONNE—EXCESSES OF MURILLO'S CORPS—
BAD NEWS—EXCHANGE OF PRISONERS—ARRIVAL BEFORE
TOULOUSE—A PRISONER OF WAR—ANECDOTE OF WEL-
LINGTON.

Head-Quarters, Samatan,
March 25, 1814.

My dear M——

At eight this morning we left L'Isle en
Dodon for this place, about eight miles nearer to
Toulouse, from which we (the head-quarters) are
now only distant about twenty-six miles.   Our
troops at St. Lys, and St. Foy, and that vicinity,
are within eleven miles ; our right is still a little
more in the rear on the St. Gaudens' road, near
Martres, under General Hill.

I have just met with a corn factor who left
Toulouse this morning.   He says Marshal Soult
arrived there with about eight thousand men last
night; the same number were expected to-day,

and a force of twelve thousand men from Suchet's army expected to join, or rather, I believe, the twelve thousand men were to be principally a reinforcement of conscripts, collected by the Imperial Commissioner Cafarelli. A small bridge called St. Antoine, near St. Martin, about a mile from Toulouse, was destroyed on the road from Isle Jourdain to Toulouse, and some works were forming, and appearance of defence making, near to St. Martin, at a place where three roads branch off a mile from Toulouse, and called La Pate d'Ore. The narrator, though no judge, thought the works could not be completed in time, and that if we pressed on we should pass them without much difficulty. The bridge he said also was mined, a very noble bridge, but it was reported that there was a ford passable so near, that it was thought the mine would not be made use of.

The news from Paris had ceased for some days, and this gave rise to many stories of Paris having been taken, &c. I am lodged here with some very civil good people, and who, I believe, really wish us well, and are very different from the maire adjoint at the last place, who seemed a good Bonapartist, as are many of the people at L'Isle en Dodon.

About six miles from that place, and ten from this, we passed through a very good old-fashioned town, larger than this, called Lombez, where the people, in spite of having had a division of troops quartered in their houses and in the church, seemed to wish us very well.

The country about here is a wide flat near the river, with a gently rising boundary of hill and good corn land, the soil heavy, and the roads very deep in consequence. I always expected my horses' shoes to be sucked off every ten minutes by the strong clay.

The maire of Boulognes continues his route with us, looking very forlorn, and with three staff corps men round him, our gens-d'armes. He began to repent to-day, and offered to act as maire, but Lord Wellington said it was too late. He then wrote to his wife, saying, " He was a martyr to his principles," &c., when his offer had been refused. So much for the principles of this good friend of Napoleon. Had his offer been accepted, he would have gone on as maire. His friend Bonaparte was, however, I really and truly think, never greater than he has been in his adversity during the last three months. The manner in which he has fought against all his difficulties is very astonishing, and I should not even now be surprised at his fighting himself into a tolerable peace. His boldness in finding fault with his generals, &c., and having them disgraced and tried at this moment, is very striking. In short, I am almost inclined to believe his own spirit, the bad conduct of the Cossacks, and the wavering policy of some of our Allies will enable him to keep his place amongst the list of sovereigns, though never to triumph over them all, as he intended, and very nearly managed to do.

There are several good chateaux near here, as I am told; one of these is occupied by Major M——, in our service, who was a prisoner of war, and thought it the best way to pass his captivity in double chains, or rather to cast off one chain by taking another, and by marrying an heiress enjoy himself whilst here. I understand he has served as maire of the place; General Pakenham and Colonel Campbell know him.

The army is now almost entirely fed on the country, and the rations paid for in bills or ready money. Our transports, such as they were, are quite outrun by our continual marches and dis-

tance from the depôts. We do not even resort
to our grand prize magazine at Mont de Marsan.
We are also boldly isolated in the country, with
scarcely five hundred men the whole way between
this and Bayonne; and between this and Tarbes
I believe none at all. Were not the general disposition of the people so good, at least so submis-
sive, the stragglers and parties joining the army,
&c., would be all destroyed; as it is, we have had
few accidents. An affair is expected in a day or
two near Toulouse, but I doubt it. In the mean-
time King Ferdinand must be in Spain, as he long
since passed through Toulouse on his way there.

9 *o'clock at night.*—Later accounts from the front
say the French are leaving Toulouse, but I think
they will make a show of resistance at least. Lord
Wellington said at dinner to-day he feared they
would blow up the bridge, but that he had his
pontoons with him, and by showing the enemy
that he could pass either above or below the
bridge, he would try and save it. To-morrow will
determine much, as head-quarters move four
leagues to St. Lys, within about three leagues of
Toulouse, and the troops are to move down into
the plain in which the town stands. This is hard

work for the men and baggage animals, as the roads are excessively deep, and I understand will be worse to-morrow than to-day. We pass through St. Foy. We cannot learn where Marshal Suchet is; Lord Wellington does not know. He received despatches by a courier from Catalonia after dinner to-day, dated the 16th of March. It was not known there for certain that he had quitted Catalonia; several here say positively that he is gone towards Lyons. I hear the post goes to-morrow early. You will probably get two or three of my letters together, as we have now no regular post-day, and I am often quartered at a distance. I do not know when the mail leaves head-quarters, and by wishing to send you the last news, I fear I may miss the post altogether.

Head-Quarters, St. Lys, March 27th, 1814.— To-day, Sunday, we make a halt here (which most of the army is very much in need of), for Lord Wellington to make arrangements and reconnoitre, &c. Four divisions are in our front, and General Hill on our right. Nothing has been done to-day but the driving in of some French pickets on this side of a little stream about two leagues from hence, and half-way to Toulouse, and we are now placed on that stream. There seemed to be but little firing. I saw it from the top of the tower of the church here, but it was soon over. From the same place the view all around was very extensive and magnificent; Toulouse was plainly visible, and much of the country beyond, together with a number of villages, chateaux, &c., in the large plain through which the Garonne takes its circular course from the Pyrenees. The snowy summits of the latter closed the prospect with their heads in the clouds.

Having had some trouble to mount to this gallery round the church, by means of the bells and their scaffolding, as there was no ladder, I was up there for two hours with my glass, in a tolerably clear and fine day. Of the importance of the latter you have no idea. Yesterday was entirely rainy, and our road was, I might almost say, as bad as any we have ever passed with artillery, and that is saying much. The troops were splashed up to their caps, and hundreds were walking barefoot in the clay up to the calves of their legs for about five miles, whilst the best of the road was like that to Hounslow in the worst season after a thaw. Lord Wellington said the French, after consultation, had determined that this road was not passable for their artillery, but by means of lighter carriages and better horses, five brigades of our guns have got over this difficulty.

To give you a notion of it I may mention that Lord Wellington's barouche was three hours fast in it at one place; one hind wheel up to the axle, the other in the air. No one was in it except General Alava, who was unwell. I left them endeavouring to move it by means of four artillery horses, in addition to his own six mules, in vain; six oxen in addition got it clear at last. Lord Wellington is gone to-day round by Plaisance to, the right, to General Hill on the Saint Gaudens' road, as that division is now approaching near us. I am always afraid of some accident in these parties in an enemy's country, as there is generally no escort—only a few officers and two or three orderlies at the most.

In a Toulouse paper of the 22nd, which I saw yesterday, I was amused with seeing, among other articles—" Bordeaux, 12th March. By accounts from this place troops without number are pouring through to join the grand army under the Duke of

Dalmatia. The disposition of the people is excellent." Then again, "March 15th. The prefect is taking measures for a number of improvements in the different communes." These lies and frauds are curious. We also see, that in publishing Soult's proclamations in the Paris papers, in which he calls Lord Wellington the commander of brigands, &c., the introductory part relating to the battle of Orthes is omitted altogether. It does not appear that any battle has taken place at all. We hope the silence as to Schwartzenburg means as much, and that the truth will be a set-off to any check given to St. Priest, &c.

Bonaparte's movements to Rheims and Chalons we cannot here comprehend. The people here, many of them, talk such bad French that I am often taken for a Frenchman, and my patron here told me I need not be afraid to own it, as he was a royalist, and always had been so. His simplicity yesterday provoked me excessively. I gave him some of my old silver spoons to take care of. Thinking all soldiers and followers of an army virtuous and honest, he left the spoons, with a loaf, in his kitchen, and left his door open, to let every one in who chose. When I returned, his loaf and my spoons were gone. I was excessively vexed, but redress was in vain.

Seisses, 28th March.—At daybreak this morning head-quarters moved to this place, most of us, I believe, fully expecting to be in Toulouse before night. We arrived here, within a league of the Garonne, by eight o'clock, when, to our great mortification, the part of the second division which had left this village at ten last night was just returning here again after daylight, owing to the bridge of boats having been too short, and the troops, therefore, unable to pass the river.

This is a most vexatious thing, as the immediate passage of the Garonne without a halt, and triumphant entry into Toulouse would have been an exploit worthy of our General. With five more pontoons the whole would have been effected, and, I believe, with little loss. In front of Toulouse the enemy had been left quiet, and pressed but little; the grand movement was to have been on the right to the banks of the river near Portet. Just below where the Arrige and the Garonne unite, a league above Toulouse, the bridge was to have been laid in the night, and half the army

over or ready to pass by daylight. The width
of the river was supposed to be about one hundred and forty yards, or four hundred and fifty
feet, the stream strong ; for this we were prepared.
The boats were in the river, the cables, I believe,
fixed, and every precaution taken for secresy,
when the discovery was made that five more pontoons would be necessary, as the river was twenty
yards, or about eighty feet wider. The boats
were all withdrawn, and the troops all in their
way to head-quarters again before daylight ; but it
was a *grand coup manqué.* Apparently there
must have been great inadvertence somewhere,
though it may have been that no measurement
was allowed, or even close observations, for fear of
exciting suspicion.

I think it will be a triumph to E——, though I
am sure he will not feel it as such. He told Lord
Wellington at St. Jean de Luz, that, in consequence of some order of his, I know not exactly
what, the pontoon train would be rendered imperfect, and that if the army met with a wide river it
would be stopped ; and thus it has happened, and
Lord Wellington, though in general so much a
gainer by his decision and resources in getting rid

of difficulties, has for once suffered for not attending to the counsel of his more steady and regularly bred scientific advisers.

As the troops were not yet ordered out of the town and were in possession of the houses, we remained for some hours with our baggage standing loaded, until our billets were settled; most part of which time I spent in surveying the immense plain covered with farms, villas, villages, towns, and chateaux, in the neighbourhood of Toulouse, as well as the town itself. The number of apparently splendid mansions was considerable, some belonging to merchants of Toulouse; some to the nobles of old, who had not emigrated; some to the *nouveaux riches* of the Revolution and Bonaparte. The latter were much abused, the fournisseurs of the army, the intendents or tax-gatherers, &c., I believe there was much fraud in the management of the collection of contributions, &c.; and of late, particularly, much more was collected under the pretence of the necessities of the army, and to provision Bayonne, than ever reached its destination; and being but ill-paid regularly, the managers took the liberty of paying themselves well irregularly.

Murillo's corps has plundered again of late, and was guilty of some excesses last night; the man was caught in the fact, stealing wine, and brought forward. Lord Wellington had him shot in the most impressive manner this morning, before all the corps, after a solemn admonition, and much parade. I am told the man appeared absolutely dead from fear before a musket was fired. He was unluckily one of the least culpable, for he had only taken away a bottle of wine by force. But he was caught in the fact, and suffered for the sake of example, as the least guilty in reality often do, from the most guilty being also the most knowing.

Lord Wellington is not yet returned; he must now exert his wits, to cure this mishap, which will not, I should think, put him in the best of humours.

The Pyrenees were to-day perfectly clear, and very striking. An immense snowy barrier almost entirely white, with scarcely any bare rock visible. They are not by any means as picturesque as the Alps. They form a large mass, without much variety of form and character; and have not that contrast of pointed, craggy fancifully shaped rocks, rounded lower hills covered with verdure, and fine forest scenery, which is seen in Switzerland.

Two of the medical officers and one of the 42nd of the sixth division, taken at Hagenau, have escaped and come in to us, but completely pillaged, and plundered of everything. The French marched them seven or eight leagues a-day, nearly thirty miles; and the one I spoke to had been concealed four days after his escape with scarcely anything to eat, until he had an opportunity of joining our corps under General Hill.

Head-Quarters, Seisses, March 31st, 1814.— Our disappointment in crossing the river on the 28th has kept us here ever since; and the halt here has given me employment, which prevented my writing to you. As soon as we are quiet, I am set to work to prevent all arrears, and to let punishment follow the offence as fast as possible.

Our General had spent his mornings in riding over the country to reconnoitre; and he dispatches all his other multitude of business at odd hours and times. The new plan was at last resolved upon, and last night the execution of it commenced. The divisions on this side Toulouse are pushed in close to the suburbs of St. Cyprian, near which the French have been, for some days, most busily at work fortifying themselves to defend the bridge. Finding the river so wide below the junction with the Arrige at Portet, General Hill (with great difficulty from the rapidity of the Garonne, owing to our last two days' continual rain) succeeded at last, in pursuance of his orders, in fixing his pontoons across that river above the junction with the Arrige, and having been nearly all night at work, began to cross about four this morning, and has sent word that he is over. A ridge of high land forms a sort of tongue between the two rivers. This he is to take post upon immediately, and march off a corps as rapidly as possible, about three leagues, to a bridge over the Arrige, which he is to surprise and preserve if possible, and defend, thus fixing himself securely between the two rivers, preparatory to further movements of the rest of the army. The Spaniards under Murillo crossed with General Hill. General Frere's Spaniards move into General Hill's ground which he leaves.

I was upon the church tower the first thing this morning, and saw the Spanish column moving all along the plain, headed by some of our heavy dragoons; the fog on the river prevented my seeing more. When I descended I found Lord Wellington and all his suite, just about to be off, when the arrival of an English mail to the 16th, stopped him. By this we have your very bad news from Holland, and many private letters accounting for the failure. All here are open mouthed at the reported consequences; namely, that the reinforcements intended for Lord Wellington are going to Holland. This is worse than the defeat. Very little was ever expected here from that army from various causes; it was always considered as so many men quite thrown away, as to the main cause. I always thought them latterly worse than inefficient, after they had once given the Dutch an opportunity of arming, by clearing their country, as they have the effect of preventing exertion on the part of the Dutch. The moment they had cleared Holland they should, I think, have been sent to us, and should thus by a sense of pressing danger, have roused the sleepy heavy Dutchmen to do something for themselves when once well in the scrape, getting only arms and artillery and stores from England.

By the exchange of prisoners, the officers so

much wanted by the French, whom Lord Wellington has taken here, will get back again by these
losses in Holland, another way in which that army
has done more harm than good.   It would have
been better to have left our people prisoners than
to release French regular officers at this moment,
as their value in the newly-raised corps is immense,
and considerably beyond that of ours to England.
Besides the numbers in the town would have has-
tened its surrender, or compelled the governor to
send them out without exchange.

This is, however, reasoning upon general principles and not upon personal feelings as to the
officers, taken ; I do think, however, this exchange
was letting humanity have more weight than
policy.   There seem to have been much blunder-
ing and confusion in the execution of our attack,
and from what I can hear the plan was allowed to
fail just when the difficulties were nearly all over.   I
am always sorry when our people are ordered to
run their heads against stone walls and heavy
guns, and that even here, as I think the French
seem to understand that work best, and we lose
more in one of these affairs than we do in gaining
a great battle in the fair field, where the French

cannot be brought now to stand against us. On this ground, I feel a little anxious, even as to Toulouse, supposing the French remain firm, of which I doubt, and still more as to Bayonne.

Mr. C—— and a commissariat officer arrived here yesterday from Bordeaux; the accounts they bring are bad enough. The National Guard are disarmed, no arming of any consequence going on, no efficient English naval force has arrived, and the people though they shout for the King at the opera, &c., are all in a terrible fright lest the French should return, as we have so small a force there, and from what I hear, many repent of what they have done.

I fear the Duc d'Angoulême is not made of stuff to gain a kingdom, though he would have kept one and been popular from his amiable qualities. He has committed many blunders, as I am told, and the white cockade gentry like the *émigrés* of old, amuse themselves with inventing lies concerning Bonaparte and his armies, which the maire of Bordeaux publishes in a bulletin, which Bonaparte's bulletins, lying as they are, effectually and satisfactorily contradict the next day.

The maire is becoming daily more unpopular.
An account we have of Augereau having been de-
feated, I hope rests upon better foundations, as
well as private accounts from Paris of the great
reduction of Bonaparte's forces by his various rapid
marches, continual fighting, and desertion.   The
only town almost in this country, excepting Bordeaux, which has been active in the Royal cause
is Bagnieres, which has proclaimed the king; no
troops of either army have passed that way.

The rest of the population in our rear are in
general only quietly waiting the event, and are now
with a very few exceptions only on our side, because
they think they see an end to the war quicker
that way; but, I am sure from what I have
seen, that let Bonaparte be successful a little and
Lord Wellington be compelled to retreat, and
let them only see the same prospect of peace by
Bonaparte's means, and three-fourths of the population would all be against us again.

The sulky maires, and other public functionaries,
now all submission, would then become active ene-
mies, and all the pensionnaires and douaniers and
national landholders who are now really frightened
to death, would be roused into activity.   This is

a picture however, I never hope to see realized, and if Toulouse and Lyons can be induced to enter into a common cause with Bordeaux, the events will I trust be far different. Had I the Duc d'Angoulême's stake to play for, I think I should somehow have raised a force before this at Bordeaux, and should certainly have been over here post to enter Toulouse, and have paraded through Pau, Tarbes, &c., in the way and tried to do something.

The only great hit he has made as yet, is to get the new prefect of the department des Landes to publish and circulate his proclamations, and sign them; this is a beginning certainly, and I hear some have found their way into Toulouse. The maire of Galan who was really I believe a royalist, pointing to his head, asked me, speaking of the Duc d'Angoulême, whether " *il y avoit quelque chose là ?*" of which he seemed to have doubts. The lower, and older population in the villages certainly, though knowing nothing of the Bourbons, have a sort of vague wish for old times again, and therefore were friendly. The middling classes are not by any means the same.

You have no conception of the obligation I have to you for sending the newspapers, &c., so regularly, and getting them forwarded in Lord Wellington's bag. On the march and in our present state, I by this means have my letters and papers sometimes a week almost before any one else; for the public bag has been lately obliged to come up, for want of transport, in a bullock car, with one weak soldier of the guides as a guard. When we are stationary I sometimes suffer by this plan, as single papers are got a day or two later than my letter, but now I am a great gainer, and my newspapers in the greatest request.

Head-Quarters, Seisses, April 1st, 1814.—Here we are still in front of " the great big town where the French are," as the Irishmen call Toulouse. The French yesterday moved about four divisions out of Toulouse after General Hill's movement, and in the evening went back again into the town. This I believe made Lord Wellington suspect that Soult intended to try an attack upon the columns of the British remaining in front of the town on this side, and he would have wished, I believe, for nothing better, as we had a rising ground commanding the roads where they must make their debouches, and cannon ready placed to give them a warm reception instantly. In consequence of this expectation Lord

Wellington and his staff were off early to the front; about eleven o'clock finding all quiet they returned here again, and we remain *in statu quo* for the day.

I must own I never expected that anything would be done if it depended on the French, as their game seems to be, only to endeavour to keep us on this side the river, and to leave us to get over the difficulties as we can, and not to run any hazards by molesting us, or giving us even a fair chance by an attack on their posts. I am told that after all, it is found that General Hill's road would lead us so much round, and that the roads round that way to Toulouse would be so bad, that the plan I mentioned (under date of the 31st) is abandoned; that in consequence General Hill will be ordered to return across the river to-night, and that the pontoons will be taken up afterwards, and an attempt made to place them lower down the river at last, and below Toulouse, which if it succeeds will place us at once upon the main good road to Bordeaux. Time will show whether this information of mine is correct. If this plan be practicable it will be far better than the other. In truth the

Garonne is a formidable barrier just now, when there are no fords.

The disappointment of not having Graham's army here is very great, much more so if the reinforcements intended for us go that way. So much did Lord Dalhousie with his weak divisions at Bordeaux expect General Graham's army, &c., that I am told he has twice sent to the coast in expectation of their arrival, together with a naval expedition, on a report of some distant sails being seen. This last gazette is a woeful contrast! The importance of that ten thousand men at Bordeaux is immense, and all agree that the country northwards would be ready to come forward to join us if we were stronger and dared advance. The weak state of our force at Bordeaux alarms them all, and keeps everything back; a naval force to co-operate and to assist against the Castle of Blaye, &c., was also expected to be ready the moment the news of our arrival at Bordeaux was received, as it must have been such a probable event. As it is, Lord Dalhousie was about to make some attempt (I understand) to take a position across the Garonne, between the Dordogne and the Garonne.

I have just been told another awkward piece of
news, if true. It is said the Duc d'Angoulême's
new *Prefêt des Landes* ordered the maire of
St. Sever to proclaim Louis XVIII., that the old
maire, a prudent, sly fellow, who has made much
money in the Revolution, declined unless by Lord
Wellington's orders, and wrote to Lord Wellington
to know if he was obliged to do what he was desired. It is said Lord Wellington replied " No,"
and suspended the new prefêt for giving the
order. This is a most awkward state of things;
each town, each maire, is allowed thus to take this
strong step if they please, but there is to be no
authority used, so that, naturally enough, all
prudent people will be quiet and do nothing, and
the desperately zealous alone will act; yet as long
as the conferences remain in existence, this cannot
be otherwise.

Some more Spaniards are ordered up whom we
are to feed also; how far they will come I know
not. The siege of Bayonne is, I understand, at
last determined upon in earnest; as yet only preparation of fascines, &c., have been made. I
am told now, the horses of the brigades of artillery
of General Hope's column, are sent down to

Renteria to bring up the heavy battery train and siege stores, &c. The Guards begin to talk of more "bloody work," but I sincerely hope not another Bergen-op-Zoom! That left column once released would set us quite at ease here. Just now, our necessarily-divided army cannot be as efficient as from its numbers compared with the French it might be presumed to be.

For fear of being too late for the post, I shall now seal up my three letters in one packet and send it off.

In appearance, the size of Toulouse is very considerable, its length particularly; it seems larger much than Bristol; whether really so or not, we have not just now conveniently the means of ascertaining.

All who come from Bordeaux are in ecstacies with the place and the life there. It seems everything a bachelor officer with a little money could wish for, everything to be had, and everything (except maps now) very cheap.

Head-Quarters, Grenade, April 5th, 1814.—In pursuance of the change of plans as to the passage of this formidable river, the Garonne, in the face of thirty thousand men, under the command of

Marshal Soult, we very suddenly moved on Sunday morning, the 3rd, to Colomiers, a poor dirty village on the high road from Auch to Toulouse. The pontoons had been previously moved in the night from near Carbonne, where they had been previously fixed, and where General Hill had passed over to the vicinity of Grenade. On the night of the 4th, about eight or nine o'clock, the whole army, excepting General Hill's columns, were put in motion towards Grenade, the pontoons were launched in the river, the bridge successfully formed during the night, and about ten thousand men passed over without resistance by daybreak. It rained furiously almost all the night, and a failure was in consequence much apprehended by many, from the increased rapidity, and breadth of the current of the river. As yet all has gone on well. General Hill's corps remained in front of the suburbs and bridge of St. Cyprien near Toulouse.

Lord Wellington and his staff were all off about two or three o'clock in the morning, or rather night, for the river side near the bridge, and passed over early in the morning. Lord Wellington reconnoitred yesterday on the right bank to within

about five or six miles of Toulouse, and did not
return here till after dark: civil departments
and baggage were ordered to move across the
country to Corn Barieu, a poor dirty place on the
cross road to Grenade, at daylight, and there to
remain loaded till further orders.   It was only four
miles of bad road, and we were there about half-
past six.   I conclude we were kept at that point
so that we might be secure, and away from the
high road, out of Toulouse, in case of accidents,
and at the same time ready to go into Toulouse, in
case the French abandoned the town and bridge
on hearing of our passage of the river, whilst on
the other hand, if they remained fast, we were
ready to come on here.

The poor mules remained loaded until nearly
two o'clock before they were ordered on, and afterwards fell in with such columns of baggage, cavalry,
and troops, particularly Spaniards, all converging to
the bridge, that they did not arrive here until about
seven or eight o'clock at night, having had to pass
a deep cross country, by a clayey unformed road,
in places sinking up to the middle, for the night's
rain and quantity of animals passing had quite cut
it up.   I left the printing-press and Mr. S——'s

carriage fast in the mud, and many a load upset; at last I believe all arrived safe.

Whilst we were waiting in suspense, as I dare not again go much to the front, Dr. M'Gregor and several other civilians and I passed our time pleasantly enough. There was a chateau on a hill near, which commanded all the country, and Toulouse in particular. To that we bent our steps, and finding a young lad, son of the owner, in the house, we got our horses into the stable, bought corn for them, and from the Doctor's canteen made a good breakfast, and then posted ourselves with our glasses to see what was going on. Had there been any fight we should have commanded the whole scene beautifully. As it was, we only traced our columns of baggage, Spaniards, and cavalry across the country, in two lines of about six or seven miles' length, all moving gradually to the bridge; we also saw some large fires in Toulouse, but have not as yet learnt whether they were anything in particular or not. About half-past one we set out again, and fought our way through mud and clay and baggage and Spaniards for about ten miles, and I am now again in a civilized home, but with rather a forward tradesman, who gave me a roast fowl for supper, but took his place and had his full share with me. It is odd enough that a man of his description, in a large good house, stables, and three or four horses, should rather boast, as he does, that he can talk French, and that his daughter of eight years old has learnt to talk French, and can speak and understand it a little when she chooses. Their patois I can scarcely make out at all, not so well as Spanish or Portuguese.

The country is all very rich and populous, and covered with villages and chateaux. The former mostly in an evident state of decay ; the latter are large and showy on the outside, but in general old, dirty, out of repair, and nearly unfurnished inside, with none of the comforts even of a cit's villa, and still less of a great man's house in England. At the same time one cannot but feel now how much of what we in England think necessaries are mere superfluity. One cause of their present appearance in part may be, that the owners generally live from seven to ten months in the year in the great towns, Toulouse in particular, and only spend September and October in their chateaux to see to the harvests, so that they, in some measure, like the Portuguese lords, when they do come, bring nearly all their furniture and comforts with them. By this means, luckily, we have not done these chateaux much damage. The young man whom we found in our chateau near Corn Barieu, had been sent out just before we arrived, to see what was going on, and to protect the place. He had not been able to have any communication with his friends in Toulouse since, and I dare say, as I told him, they were in a terrible fright, and thought the Spaniards had roasted and eaten him up.

Last night it unfortunately rained again all night. This has swelled the river, and alarmed us a little, as there are at times such floods here that our bridge would not stand them, and we are now half on each side. This was also very unlucky for the troops, who must many of them have bivouacked without their tents and baggage. I have heard as yet of no ill consequences, and it is thought the French must either come out and fight us immediately, or be off and leave us at our ease for a short time to try and refit and get shoes for our poor barefooted soldiers, &c. In the mean time we are here with no other orders than to be ready packed to march from ten o'clock, but not loaded. It is now half-past ten, and I have been quietly writing this, and four letters on business, since breakfast.

The last day I was at Seisses I met at Lord Wellington's Major M——, of the 53rd, the *ci-devant* prisoner and French squire, whom I mentioned before in my letters. He was at Toulouse when we came by his former house, and he took the opportunity of our bridge (of pontoons) at Carbonne to come out, and over to us, or rather to come over; for to go out he was compelled.

I do not quite understand his own story, so as to make his conduct correct. He was always on a sort of parole in Languedoc and Gascony. On our coming near Toulouse he was told he must retire towards Montpelier; he asked delay, on the plea of health, got a day, was then ordered to move post by Carcassonne. He went two stages, then turned to the right, came over to us, and now rides about, a strange figure, in a new handsome 53rd uniform, and a great French cocked-hat, with his English loop and button. He is, moreover, a round broken-backed country-squire volunteer sort of gentleman, on a high white tumble-down French nag. He was of course full of information and conversation, but I rather doubted the accuracy of the former.

He told us Bonaparte was making for Metz, giving up Paris, and that he intended to relieve his garrisons in that direction even as far as Wesel, and then to try to bring the war to the frontier again. This would be giving up nearly all France, and putting himself between the Crown Prince at Liege and the Allies near Paris, whereas, I think, if compelled to leave Paris, his line must be to back towards Lyons, and to try and unite in that direction with Augereau, and even with Soult, who will, I think, fall back that way also. If Bonaparte were to go to Metz, Lord Wellington said he thought then the Allies, on entering Paris, would probably let the King be proclaimed, and that he should not then despair of seeing Bonaparte a grand Guerilla chief on a large scale, fighting about for his existence, which he had never expected to happen in his life-time. Major M——— also said that Soult's plan was, if obliged to give up Toulouse, to go towards the Black Mountains, and retreat by way of Carcassonne, making his stand there in a country where our superior cavalry could not act. If he does this, I think half his men will

desert, and the remainder be in jeopardy, unless
Suchet brings him more assistance than is thought
possible. Suchet is said to be withdrawing everything, and to be mustering all he can. Oh that
we had your English reinforcements, and General
Graham's army! as our own real English army
dwindles away very fast in this active service, and
ten thousand men may make all the difference in
the event. The 53rd regiment and the eighteen-
pounders are, I hear, hutted at Tarbes, to go and
try to reduce a small garrison at Lourdes. The
Householders are also arrived, I believe, as far as
Tarbes.

On the 23rd of March, Caffarelli sent his orders
to all the communes round Toulouse, for a considerable distance, about fifty communes, to send
men to work at the fortifications in front of
Toulouse. The numbers to be sent by requisition
were very considerable, but we have rather disturbed
the march of the larger half. He also called upon
all the inhabitants to arm and to make the town
a second Saragoza.

Major M—— says he was told there was not
the same motive. I understand they have been
obliged to arm by compulsion, but it is supposed

will do nothing. Some old French officers also
came to Soult to offer to raise Guerillas corps in
our rear. Major M—— said their offers were to
be accepted, but, except a few for plunder, I do
not think, as yet, they will find many followers.
Lord Wellington makes the maires responsible
for any disturbances in the rear, and threatens
garrisons, as on the French plan, *garnissaires,* in
case of a breach of order. To execute this duty the
maires are allowed to arm guards in their communes. All the communes around here were to
have *garnissaires* in case the workmen did not
arrive—that is, soldiers to keep in their houses
gratis.

One o'clock same day.—Here we are still, and I
hope shall not move to-day, unless to go into
Toulouse, as there is a report that the French are
moving off now, and that we have taken two cars
of money. This, I will not vouch for. What is
more certain, I believe, is, that our pontoon bridge
is on its legs again by land, and moving towards
Toulouse, to be laid down nearer the town, to
make our communications shorter between our
two parts of the army, on the right and left bank.
I fear this may draw head-quarters into some little

dirty village near the bridge, and I should like to enjoy a tolerable clean brick room which I have to myself, and a little stable with some hay for my horses, for one day, if it suits our plans.

At first I was surprised at Major M——'s boldness, and I thought folly, in going about in his uniform, in a way to do no good to anybody, and possible harm to himself. I have now heard that he has been divorced from his lady, and of course, by the French law, from his *château* and *terre* also, and that now he has nothing whatever to lose. He may as well make a merit of his love of England and the Bourbons. His daughter, about sixteen, is married, and the property goes with her. A party of five dragoons took yesterday a messenger from Montauban to Soult. It was known by eleven o'clock at Montauban, that we had cut off the communications on the main road. The messenger was sent round a bye road, but was caught. I am told his despatches were principally complaints that the people would not arm for the fight, and were not very material. I pitied the man. He was a respectable man of business in Montauban, but being told that unless he became a civic soldier he must be a regular, he put on his sword, &c., "by compulsion," was sent to carry these letters, and thus fell into our hands. He says it will be his ruin to send him to England as a prisoner, and I hope, though he is threatened with this, that Lord Wellington will soon release him. I hope this, believing from what I have heard, his story to be true, as the Prefêt of Montauban is reported to be a most furious Bonapartist, and that he arms the people in the cause even by threatening their lives, till they wear them. All here profess great friendship for us, and I believe, at present are sincere.

Six o'clock.—About two o'clock I saw Lord Wellington come in, and the real news was, that all was quiet on both sides the river, but that the floods had carried away or sunk one pontoon, and that the bridge was impassable. It was just on the point of being moved higher when this happened. Just now, it is not safe to place it anywhere. We have only three divisions and three brigades of artillery across, and two or three, I believe, of cavalry. The Spaniards are not over, as I supposed, but were to have gone over this morning. Unless Soult is an arrant coward, he now must attack these men, and I fear we shall have sharp

work.   A position, however, may be taken near
the river, so as to enable our artillery on this side
to assist.   The river has fallen above a foot since
morning, as it has hitherto been fine to-day, but
I am sorry to say it has now begun to rain again,
and looks very much like another bad night.
Rain upon the present river would be tremendous.
A quarter of an hour after Lord Wellington came
home from Toulouse, I met him going off again to
cross the river; I therefore conclude something
important had happened.

6th of April, 9 *o'clock at night. Head-
Quarters at Grenade.*—My principal occupation
to-day, when not engaged by business, has been to
watch the river.   It continued to fall many hours
after our last rain had ceased, and began to rise
at ten to-day, about fifteen hours after the last
rain commenced, and five after it ceased; at this
rate it will continue to rise until six or eight to-
night, and then fall again; and if the weather
relent a little, I think to-morrow our bridge will be
restored.

Marshal Soult has left our three divisions quite
quiet on the other site.   If he knows their numbers,
this is playing the game of a coward.   At present

he seems to think of nothing but fortifying Toulouse with ditches and works, and his men are hard at work. This makes the delay very unfortunate for us. It has, indeed, been so on every account, as we have to-day received accounts which appear to be believed, that twelve hundred French cuirassian cavalry, from Suchet's army, joined yesterday, and that time is what he is endeavouring to gain, and what the elements favour his obtaining.

The only two events here to-day have been first the arrival of the pontoon, which was lost and floated away. Lieutenant Reid, of the Engineers, galloped to Verdan, two leagues down the river, offered a reward of *cent francs*, or five pounds, to any inhabitants who would get boats and stop the pontoon and bring it ashore. The deserter was thus secured, and to-day brought back in triumph by a party of soldiers. The other arrival astonished us all. A troop of the Royal Horse Guards Blue arrived with drawn swords and a Captain's guard escorting a carriage. Some said it was the Duc d'Angoulême, some one great person, some another. One officer asked the Captain if it was King Ferdinand? This was a hoax. At last it was discovered to be a maire of a small commune near Tarbes, and his wife. The maire is supposed to have been endeavouring to favour a guerilla system, and exciting the people to arm. He was in consequence ordered to be sent to head-quarters; and the manner of putting the order into execution it is concluded was entirely the act of General O—— and his Householders, who supposed, I conclude, they were escorting Sir Francis Burdett to the Tower of London. It has been a good joke, but the Blues were in high condition; and Lord Wellington, when he was told of the French cuirassiers, said, " Well, then, we must have the Householders for these gentlemen, and see what they can make of them."

I must tell you two little anecdotes as to the pontoon bridge. The French were very jealous of any attempt of the kind, and had cavalry videttes, &c., all along their banks of the river. The engineer wished to measure the breadth of the river at the spot intended; he got into conversation with the French vidette a long time, but had no opportunity. At last he pretended that the calls of nature were imperative. The Frenchman, out of decency, withdrew. The engineer popped out his sextant, took the angle, &c., and was off.

Lord Wellington himself with two other officers went to the spot also to reconnoitre with his own eyes. Concealing his General's hat with an oil-skin, he got into conversation with the French vidette, dismounted, got down to the water-side, looked all about him, saw all he wished, and came away. I think this was risking too much; but no French soldier would have any idea of the commander of the allied forces going about thus with two attendants. Lord Wellington was yesterday over alone on foot, and went on upon a horse of General Cole's, as horses could not pass. Even General P—— was a little uneasy, and sent about eight o'clock to know if he had come back safe. He returned about seven o'clock, when it was dusk. To-day he has a great dinner in honour of Badajoz.

7th April, Grenade.—We have at last a fine clear day, and warm. The river is falling rapidly. By this evening I think our bridge may be re-established, and to-morrow I conclude we shall pass more troops and advance against Toulouse and the

French marshal, who is digging and working away as usual. The French made several attempts to destroy our bridge before the floods did the business for them. They sent us down all their dead horses, several trees, &c., and a large old boat, which struck a pontoon and went down itself instead of the pontoon. They sent down also a sort of armed log stuck round with swords, and rolling round and round in the stream as it went along, like a great fish, in hopes that the swords would strike and cut the cable which holds the boats.

Major M. M—— has just told me he has had news from the interior of another defeat of Bonaparte at Arcis sur Aube, and of his having lost one hundred guns, &c., and being then manœuvring in the rear of the Allies. This seems probable. He has also an account of the departments in the west of France, having all sent in to the Duc d'Angoulême at Bordeaux for orders—this is also probable and that the Royalists gain ground fast. His accounts add in the postscript,—" The Allies entered Paris April 1st." This ought to be, I think, from former accounts, and I hope it is so. The last *Moniteur* we have of the 30th talks of Bonaparte's return to Paris to cover the city. How he could then get there seems the difficulty. Lord Wellington also had yesterday a private letter from the interior, in which it is said, *" un événement bien imprévu est arrivé à Paris,"* and no comment. He guesses it to be the flight of the Empress. You see what confused accounts we get of all late events ?

7th (6 *o'clock.*)—In addition to the above we have now the news that the Bourbons have been proclaimed at Paris, and that in the name of the Emperor of Austria the house of Napoleon has been declared to cease to reign. I must now seal up, as Lord Wellington has written his English letters to-day, Thursday, although Saturday is the usual day. In addition to this, I think we shall move to-morrow, from many symptoms.

P.S.—The maire brought in with such a magnificent escort is now quietly walking about here with his wife and no guard. The bridge is to be fixed nearly in the same place again to-night.

CHAPTER V.

Head-Quarters, Grenade,
April 10, 1814, 1 o'clock.

MY DEAR M——

HERE we are still, away from all that is
going on, but expecting every moment an order to
enter Toulouse. The day before yesterday the
bridge was re-established (the 8th), and by one
o'clock the Spaniards had all passed over. The
order then came for a brigade of Portuguese artillery to do the same; they were passing when I went
there, soon after one o'clock, and just as a gun
was quitting the last boat to ascend the bank, down
went the boat; the gun, however, run off safe, but
two of the Portuguese pontoon train sailors got

a ducking, which was all the mischief except a delay of about two hours to fish up the pontoon, drag it on shore, turn it upside down, to clear out the water, and then launch it again, and refit the board, &c.

By four o'clock I left the remainder of the guns going over. The head-quarters of Lord Wellington remained at St. Jouy that night, and last night Lord Wellington has only pushed the troops on a little to reconnoitre, and in the evening the 18th Hussars, under Colonel Vivian, had a brilliant affair. They charged the French cavalry on the high-road, broke them, sabred several, and took about seventy prisoners, with the loss of a few officers wounded, and, I believe, only about six or eight men; unluckily, Colonel Vivian received a ball in the arm, which, it is feared, will render amputation necessary. Yesterday (the 9th), the bridge was taken up very early, and ordered to be fixed immediately about four miles nearer the town of Toulouse, at a little place called Assaic. The light divisions were close to that point on this side of the river, as a security in case of any attack on the second division, near St. Cyprien and the bridge of Toulouse. They were ordered to cross the river as soon as our pontoons were ready, and a movement was intended, and ordered yesterday.

From some difficulties or bad management, the bridge of boats was not ready until nearly three o'clock, when it was thought too late. Lord Wellington was more vexed, and in a greater state of anger, than he usually is, when things go wrong, even without any good cause. He said his whole plans for the day were frustrated and nothing could be done; and the light divisions were counter-ordered to remain where they were on this side the river, and head-quarters remained at St. Jouy.

The French it appeared (still keeping a force to defend the bridge of Toulouse), had, before this, taken a strong position, on the hills beyond the town, and had made there some strong works, upon which they were constantly busy. The last two days and nights their main body rested on the hills bivouacking in this position, and in an uncomfortable state, hourly expecting an attack. This morning about seven it commenced; the firing was heavy for about two hours, until nine, and has continued partially since. As I dare not cross the river and go to the front I went with my glass to the highest look out here, and saw the French redoubt very plainly, firing away briskly; since that all has been silent here, and free from smoke. The stories here from the people are that, with the loss of six thousand men, we have taken the redoubt and thirty-six pieces of ordnance.

The former, from the direction of the fire, I am sure is a lie, and perhaps the latter. As, however, we have now some sort of official news that the Allies are in Paris, and the Imperial Court at Orleans, and as there is no account of Bonaparte, I think the French here will not fight much; and if beaten I am sure many, nay thousands, will run home, and the army be much diminished. I suspect Bonaparte will try to unite his corps and all the remains of corps near Paris, and Augereau's from Lyons, and Marshal Soult's and Suchet's from Provence, towards Montpelier; but I am in hopes even regiments, and perhaps Marshals, will begin to desert when it is found Paris is taken, and the royal party proclaimed and gaining ground.

We certainly are in a very odd state just now in France. Our military chest, Paymaster, Doctors, Commissaries, &c., and nearly all our money are in

this place, altogether without troops; only about a
dozen staff corps men, and about ten of the paymaster's ordinary marching guard. The army all
in front, nearly four leagues, our only protection
the good-will of the people, and the river, and yet
we are told there are French troops at Montauban,
about four leagues off, and nothing between us except the river. All feel, notwithstanding, quite
secure, and have no anxiety but to enter Toulouse.

In the mean-time Lord Dalhousie with a part
of the seventh division has crossed, not only the
Gironde, but the Dordogne, and, we are told, is to
take Fort Blaze by storm; I suppose his whole
force is not above three thousand five hundred men.
Bayonne has not yet been seriously attacked, nor
do we hear of any very great distress in the town,
which I am surprised at, from the length of the
blockade.

I am told, in the attack to-day the third and
sixth divisions were to form the right of the attack on
the river, the fourth the centre, and the light and
large body of Spaniards to make the flank movement on the left, to get on the hills and turn the
French position, whilst the cavalry advance also in

that direction, to be ready to take advantage of the enemy's retreat.

5 o'clock, same day.—No one returned, and no news; and yet no firing heard, and no orders. I fear the resistance has been greater than was expected, and I begin to be fidgety and uneasy. The reports are now eight thousand English wounded, and fighting in the streets now going on. If such complete ignorance of the truth exists within ten miles of what is passing, you may judge how false reports circulate; we receive contradictory ones every hour. All we know for certain is, that two hours ago Lord Wellington's baggage remained at St. Jouy without orders; I despair, therefore, of seeing Toulouse to-day, and am going to dinner instead.

Grenade, April 11th, 8 o'clock, morning.—The firing continued all day yesterday, and until past eight at night, and began again at four this morning, and has continued to this time, but has now lessened. Several of our civilians returned home here last night. I understand our loss is very considerable. We drove the enemy from all the heights, but with difficulty. The Spaniards failed in the attack of a redoubt, were put to the rout

completely, and, I understand, would have lost
their guns, which the French were within two or
three hundred yards of, had not the Portuguese
stepped in to their support, and enabled them to
rally again.

This is really too bad—my friend says the ground
was covered with dead Spaniards, and he saw but
few French; this is generally the result of alarm
and flight. The redoubt was taken, but not by
the Spaniards, as I hear; the fire close to Lord
Wellington was most severe. Near the town the
French fought very hard in the houses, particularly
at some houses near the lock of the canal close to
the river. We each occupied some of the houses,
and fired continually; the French houses were
loop-holed, and they had the best. We were
obliged to bring guns, &c.; and, unfortunately, the
most successful shell fell into one of our own
houses, and burnt out our own people. Among
the killed, &c., I hear, is Colonel Coghlan of the
61st — an excellent officer, Lieutenant-colonel
Forbes, Captain Gordon, 10th Hussars. Colonel
Fitzclarence is wounded in the thigh; he charged
with his troops two French squadrons (as he says
himself) up a hill, beat them, but, on the top, was

received by infantry: the first shot carried away part of his sword, the second hit him on the thigh, and they fell back. We were close to the town and to the bridge last night on all sides, and had moved our bridge up within two miles of the town. The French have barricaded the houses and streets, fixed swivels on the tops, lined the roofs with men, &c., and seem determined to defend the town with desperation. An officer deserted yesterday, and says he will serve no longer under a man who acts like a madman, as Soult now does in defending a town like Toulouse in such a manner.—It is madness.

Four Spanish officers came in here yesterday, who had escaped from Italy through Switzerland, and had walked here. They seemed in great distress. We had no Commissary here: I therefore gave them eight pounds of bread and a dozen eggs, got them a quarter for the night, and advised them to stay here until this morning, and then proceed to head-quarters. One had served in Colonel Roche's corps in Catalonia, and spoke English tolerably. Our delay here, and in taking the town, has alarmed the people very much. All who have relations and friends in Toulouse are terribly

frightened.   The officer who deserted says many
will do the same as soon as the business is over,
and occasions arise.   Captain O. K——, the
French-English officer from Toulouse, who came
over to the Duc d'Angoulême, at St. Jean de Luz,
arrived here yesterday from Bordeaux.   He says
things are going on well, especially since the
Paris business; that the Duke has now eighteen
hundred men formed; and that French officers
come in every day with fleurs-de-lys embroidered
on their Napoleon uniforms, and thus tender their
services.   O. K—— was here on his road to Au-
rillac, to Auvergne, &c., where, he says, a party
is formed and ready to rise.   He must take care
of his head, as he goes about talking very impru-
dently.

Head-Quarters, Toulouse, April 13, 1814, *Sec-
tion* 3, *No.* 676.—To give you any notion of
what we have all felt from the changes which the
last thirty-six hours have produced, I must take
you back to my first sheet, and I am sure you will
feel more as I did, by reading in succession what
has occurred, than by anything I can now write.
I was about to destroy the first sheet, as much of
it is now not worth the trouble of reading; but I

thought it would give you a better idea of our daily feelings with the army.

An order came for civil departments to march, to cross the pontoons, and to proceed on the high road to Toulouse to a church only three miles from the town, and there halt and wait for orders. We were off in ecstacies, expecting all to dine in Toulouse, and that the French were off, and our men after them. Judge of our vexation, when, on arriving at the church, we were all turned back off the road to a miserable village of about ten houses, called St. Albains; and were there to find quarters for the night, in places just quitted by the plundering Spaniards, and left nearly in the state the French left the houses in Spain as they passed.

When we arrived, we found many of the Spaniards still in possession, and four of us disarmed and seized three of them in the act of plundering. The people were screaming in every direction, the houses abandoned, and the inhabitants just beginning to return to witness the mischief done—everything had been ransacked—all the closets, &c., broken open—the rags and remnants on the floor, mixed with hundreds of egg-shells, and the feathers of the plundered fowls, &c. Much linen was carried off, the sheets, and heavy articles in the yard; the tables were covered with broken dishes, bottles, bones, and twine; and the cellars with the wine casks running. In about two hours we got possession of the quarters, and got the inhabitants in to clean them, &c., and, by five, had divided the places among us. My whole baggage lost its road, and did not arrive at all— five mules and a horse loaded. Luckily, Mr. and Mrs. D——, (for she was in one poor farmhouse) gave me some dinner; and, after a melancholy conversation with Dr. M'Gregor, the principal medical officer, I went to bed.

You may conceive the disappointment and the vexation. Dr. M'Gregor said our loss was terrible! He was just returned from collecting all the wounded in villages, and, by Lord Wellington's desire, was hurrying every one possible instantly to the rear. They were passing all night in cars. The Spaniards were moaning and crying most desperately, to reach Fenoullet that night, Sole Jourdain the next, and then to be sent on further if necessary. The accommodations were very bad. The accounts from the town were that the French were continuing to barricade every house and loophole, arming to defend themselves to the last.

The army was said to be now much weakened; the Spaniards could not be depended upon; the reinforcements were not come up from England, and a story was going about and believed by many who ought to have known better, that we were out of our ammunition, and could not use our artillery. You may conceive that I went (without my baggage and comforts), with this news, sorrowfully to bed, ordering my servant to be off at five in the morning in search of my stragglers.

On the 12th, at six o'clock, I was up and wandering about alone, listening to an occasional heavy gun, seeing wounded men pass, and waiting for the return of my man, without the means of getting shaved or breakfast. About eight I saw Henry returning alone, and was expecting more bad news, when he told me the French were off, that we were to march for Toulouse directly, and that my baggage was all safe at a house a league off on the road; and that, therefore, he had ordered them to pack, and be off with the rest. Think of our sensations on hearing of this welcome change! The last twenty-four hours had been among the most critical of the war, and now all was safe and right again. I found out the clergyman, Mr. B——, got a razor and a cup of tea, whilst my horse was getting ready, and was then off, to go round by head-quarters and to enter Toulouse with Lord Wellington. About eleven I arrived at the fortified entrance, and found, instead of the enemy behind the new works, the maire of the town, all the officers almost of the guarde urbaine, a considerable number of national guard officers, deserters, &c., and about two hundred smart but awkward men of the city guard, and a band of music, all with the white cockade, and a great crowd of citizens besides, all waiting with anxiety to receive Lord Wellington, and carry him in form to the mayoralty. Unluckily, from some mismanagement and mistake, he went in at another entrance, and passed on, almost unknown. I heard this, and went to the mayoralty with General Pakenham's aide-de-camp, found it was so ; and, therefore, we went back to inform the mayor officially, and to beg he would return to the *maison commune*. He did so, though an immense crowd entered the mayoralty in form, and an introduction then took place, and Lord Wellington showed himself at the window, amidst the shouts and waving hand-kerchiefs and hats of every one.

The procession then went with Lord Wellington to his quarters, the Prefêt's palace, amidst the applause of the inhabitants all the way. Nothing could be more gratifying than his reception, and that, indeed, of all the English; the most respectable inhabitants, many of them, not only anxiously showing us the way to our billets, but offering their homes without any billets, or receiving us with a sincere welcome as soon as the paper was delivered. Lord Wellington announced a ball in the evening at the Prefecture, and left Marshal Beresford with three divisions and cavalry to follow Marshal Soult for the day.

We thought nothing could make us happier, when at five o'clock in came Colonel Ponsonby from Bordeaux with the Paris news, which you know. He told us that the official accounts would arrive in an hour or two. Ponsonby came through Montauban; the French officer commanding there taking his word, and letting him pass. I had been, at Colonel Campbell's request, examining General St. Hilaire and his servant. St. Hilaire was found, under suspicious circumstances, in the town, and was just put under arrest, and Campbell luckily asked me to dine with Lord Wellington, which I should have been very sorry to have missed.

Just as we were sitting down to dinner—about forty of us—General Frere, and several Spaniards, General Picton, and Baron Alten, the principal French, &c., in came Cooke with the despatches. The whole was out directly, champagne went round, and after dinner Lord Wellington gave "Louis XVIII.," which was very cordially received with three times three, and white cockades were sent for to wear at the theatre in the evening. In the interim, however, General Alava got up, and with great warmth gave Lord Wellington's health, as the *Liberador del' Espagna!* Every one jumped up, and there was a sort of general exclamation from all the foreigners, French, Spanish, Portuguese, Germans, and all — *El Liberador d'Espagna! Liberador de Portugal! Le Libérateur de la France! Le Libérateur de l'Europe!* And this was followed, not by a regular three times three, but a cheering all in confusion for nearly ten

minutes! Lord Wellington bowed, confused, and
immediately called for coffee. He must have been
not a little gratified with what had passed.

We then all went to the play. The public were
quite in the dark as to what had just arrived, but
Lord Wellington was received in the stage-box
(where he sat supported by Generals Picton, Frere,
and Alava, &c., and also the maire), with no
little applause, I can assure you. At the door the
people would scarcely take the money from us;
and in the opposite stage-box the French left the
box themselves, and made room for us. We had
our white cockades on the breast. The English
officers in the house stared, and did not know what
to make of it. Some thought it a foolish, giddy
trick. In about ten minutes Lord Wellington turned
his hat outwards to the front of the box: it was
seen, and a shout ensued immediately. The play
was "*Richard, oh mon Roi*,"—fixed upon really
before the news came. The "*Henri IV.*" was
played, and then the new French Constitution was
read aloud from one of the boxes. The people most
anxious,—in general, pleased; in some things not
I own I think most of it very good, if the French
can enjoy anything so like our own constitution,

as it is, under other names; but I am doubtful of this. The article worst received was that leaving all the sales of emigrant lands to stand good; and I certainly think, when, by means of paper, an estate had been bought for the price of a team of horses, an equitable arrangement would have been better, to be settled by Government Commissioners. This was followed by " God save the King," which was received with great applause.

When the play was over, we adjourned to the ball at Lord Wellington's. The only drawback was our meeting, on the way, the cars of the wounded in the streets, now moving to the excellent hospitals here. This, on consideration, was also a satisfaction, as many lives will be saved, by the wounded being here, instead of being sent to the rear. You will now, I think, guess what we felt, and what a species of trance we were in.

Here we are halted, whilst the news is sent on to Soult, with whom Marshal Beresford could not come up. The arrival of the news was at the moment we should have selected, except for the loss of life. For Lord Wellington's character, however, even that was good, and eight hours sooner it would have been said our late battle was no victory, and that we should never have entered Toulouse, nor would the real sentiments of the town have been known.

On inquiry, I find the French loss has been great. General Tausen, one of my friends on La Rune, killed; General D'Armagnac, who took me, wounded; Harispe wounded, and here a prisoner; two other Generals wounded, &c. Our loss fell principally, you will see, on the sixth division, and the Scotch Brigade in particular, and on the Spaniards. With regard to the latter, I am told, upon the whole the men for a long time behaved well, and that if General Frere had been as skilful as brave, and the officers better, they probably would have succeeded in their object, which certainly happened to be the most arduous duty of the day. They arrived on a sort of smooth glacis under the French works, subject to a fire admitted to be more severe than almost any since Albuera. Decision and skill and rapidity were then required. The men were kept too long in this fire—they broke—and then ran like sheep. One French regiment, I understand, drove four thousand of them and more, and in such a manner that they almost upset a Caçadore Portuguese regiment by main force. Three companies of the latter stood firm, beat back the Spaniards with their firelocks, laughed at them, enjoyed it, and checked the French completely. The redoubt was afterwards taken by our people, with great loss, as you will see. General Frere was in despair; he exerted himself to the utmost to rally his men; at last, by the exertions he made, assisted by Lord Wellington in person, one or two Spanish companies were formed, and became steady. Upon these the rest soon followed, and formed up also. The Spaniards had a less arduous post assigned them, all went on well again, and I believe they behaved fairly enough. Their loss is considerable.

This morning the whole conversation of the officers turns upon half-pay and starvation. With some, want of preferment; with others, promotion; and with those who have promotion, a determination to enjoy themselves now all is over, and their dangers and sufferings past. As to my own prospects, they are so completely in the air; that as I never was much of an architect for building in that element, I go quietly on with my work, and trust to the future.

I shall defer any account of this place, &c., for

fear of being too late for the despatches, and now say adieu.

Pray forward the enclosed two letters, which are from Madame de Baudré, my hostess at Mont de Marsan, who desired me to take care of them, and enclosed them in a letter of great professions of kindness for me, only exceeded by the most romantic ones for the Bourbons, and stating the great losses her family and connexions have lately sustained.

Head-Quarters, Toulouse, April 15*th,* 1814.—Here we are quietly waiting the result of the communication of the late news to Marshal Soult, &c. Cooke has come back from his head-quarters. The Marshal hesitates at present, a little. He objects that he has no authentic documents from Bonaparte, or the authorities whom he represents, and seems to have some doubts of the extent of the late news—or pretends this. In short, as yet he takes no decided line, but I believe has applied for an armistice, I suppose wishing to gain time, to consult Suchet, &c., and learn more of the state of things.

Colonel Gordon was sent to him yesterday by Lord Wellington with a flag-of-truce; and it is understood a positive answer and determination was required, and the armistice refused. Lord Wellington and all the officers yesterday attended Colonel Coghlan's funeral in the morning, at the Temple, and went from thence in procession to the Protestant burial-ground out of the town.

In the evening Lord Wellington gave another more magnificent ball at the Prefecture. It was too crowded to dance much, or well, but went off with great glee and general satisfaction. The ladies. were very prettily dressed, in general, with the exception of a few of the high ugly bonnets, and there were several very pleasing looking girls, and good dancers; but I do not think that in general the women are handsome here. I met with one very good humoured chatty lady, about eighteen I should suppose, who said she had only left her " Maman," with whom she had always lived near Carcassonne, one month, and that, in that time she had witnessed many strange things:—the ravages of the French army, the passage of our army over the Garonne, a great battle (which was all visible quite plainly from the churches here, and even from the houses), the preparations for a siege, the retreat of the French, our triumphal entry, the change of the national government and her own marriage !

Captain Tovey of the 20th, taken at Orthes, has escaped, and came in here yesterday; he would not give his parole, and made several attempts to be off; in consequence, he has been hardly treated, but is now safe. He met with every assistance from the French inhabitants : and at the last house he was in, the owner made him leave all his peasant's dress, and equipped him in a new suit, boots and all, French cut, to pass our lines and go to head-quarters in. The villages he passed were proclaiming the King; and he was told that Soult's house, near Carcassonne, had been destroyed by the mob.

The French here show the volatile character as much as ever. *Vive le Roi* is shouted as vigorously as *Vive l'Empereur* was, I am told, a few years since, when Bonaparte made his then really popular entry, and gave his fêtes here, of which the most fulsome *procès verbal* still exists, signed by a maire-adjoint of the same name as the one who now signs the King's proclamation, and I believe he is the same man—Lameluc.

The inhabitants are all at work as usual, and

very active. Fleurs de lis are now upon the skirts of the coats instead of eagles, and last night, on the theatre drop-scene. The busts of Bonaparte are smashed. The Capitolium ornaments are all undergoing a change. All the N.'s and B.'s, &c., are effaced; and the workmen are now busily employed working round the cornice of the great staircase at the Capitol, in changing all the alternate ornaments of a handsome cornice, every other one having been a *bee*. The English are everything and in general estimation. To return the compliment of our wearing their white cockade on our black one, they now wear a black one on their white. The Spaniards are considered much as the Cossacks. The Capitolium is a very fine building, and as the splendid velvet and gold canopy and the throne of Bonaparte at one end had no decided emblems except that of authority generally, it has, after some doubts, been allowed to remain, and is not destroyed. We are to have a grand ball there, I am told, given on Sunday by the inhabitants, if approved of, and we stay.

The theatre is about the size of the Haymarket Theatre in width, rather larger, but much deeper, and something in the improved shape of Covent

Garden. The actors are tolerable. It is, however, inferior I believe to the Bordeaux Theatre, and certainly to that of Lyons.

The stone bridge over the Garonne, of seven arches, is very solid and substantial, wide, and upon the whole, a splendid work, but not very graceful in its architecture. It is like Kew bridge in general shape, but in much heavier and substantial proportions.

Several improvements have been some time since, commenced in the city, but most of them are now at a stand, and have been so for some time. The cathedral St. Etienne is an unfinished Gothic building, the great aisle being wanting of the new building; and instead of it, a large sort of Westminster Hall of more ancient date, which joins it on one side, crooked, and was intended originally to be pulled down or altered.

There is some good tapestry and fine painted glass, which has escaped here, as in several other churches, the revolutionary destruction.

The streets here are like the old parts of Paris, in general narrow, with a gutter in the middle: and the houses very good, but high shops below, and three stories of good rooms above. Several

handsome hotels, with their great gates and small
gardens. I am in a dirty place, but tolerably well
off. The hotel I am in is to let, and therefore in
bad order, and I have in consequence no respectable owner. The people in it are civil; I have
good stabling, and one comfortable room, now it is
cleaned.

C—— gives rather a strange account of our allies,
but seems to think from their numbers, and the
general feeling, the business has at last been well-
blundered through. There is a good story told of
an incident which happened at the interview
with Soult the other day. The substance of the
news somehow got wind, and the army, whilst the
Marshal was closeted with C——, gave a loud
shout. The aide-de-camp went to inquire the
cause, and returned saying, " *Ce n'est qu'un lièvre,*
Monseigneur." You ought to know that nothing
causes a louder shout amongst troops than a hare
crossing them. General M—— said the aide-de-
camp should have been asked whether it was a
Leipsic hare? If Soult does not declare himself,
his army will, I think, desert him. I have now
but just received a letter from you, of the 22nd
March, and papers.

The French works at the entrance of the town, by the bridge (the *tête de pont*), were very strong, and cost much in labour and materials, for no use. They were formed by close piles of timber like the caissons for the foundation of a bridge, filled up with earth, and the tops lined by barrels of earth, with a ditch and guns, &c., placed, and the walls of the buildings round all loopholed.

I also rode all over the position of the battle yesterday, on the hills, and examined all the forts and the monuments of French industry and British courage : they were most formidable places to approach, as the hills formed a regular smooth glacis from the works at the top to the valley below, and half way down were long low heaps of sod, or turf, made up to protect the advanced sharpshooters, who were lying safe on the ground behind them protected, though the barrier was not above two feet high. A church and a house loopholed, formed the sort of citadel to two of the forts or redoubts for musketry, with the guns around the outside. The ditches were not as deep, nor the works as complete as those near Vera, where the French had more time, nor were the roads or mountains so difficult to ascend ; but there was less shelter to approach from the greater smoothness of the ground. The only chance of safety almost was following up some hollow roads, and a ride or two on the hills.

16*th* (4 *o'clock*).—I have just heard the mail goes in half an hour. I have, therefore, little time to add to this. Colonel G—— is come back: Soult very civil, but high and proud in his manner, not yet satisfied, and so circumstanced, does not yet join the royal cause; the consequence is, I hear, that the troops move to-morrow morning, and I fear we will do the same then or soon after. This is very provoking, as the general result seems clear, and all bloodshed now useless. I suspect the truth of the hare story, as it is said that Soult's army is still ignorant of what has happened, at least nearly so. Pains are now taking to circulate the proclamations, news, &c. &c., in all directions round him, that the troops may learn the real state of things. I have to-day received the parcel from you, letter to 29th, newspapers, &c. Many thanks, but I have no time to answer the contents.

The Museum here contains but a bad second-rate set of pictures. About a hundred have been carried away during the month of March, no one knows where; but I presume they were the best of those which were portable from their size.

There has been some difference of opinion, and confusion, we hear, at Montauban, about royalty. Bayonne, I fear, will abide by Soult, and do nothing yet.

Head-Quarters, Toulouse, April 18*th,* 1814, 5 *o'clock.*—The troops moved as I told you yesterday, and the order was actually out for headquarters moving to-day, when Count Gazan came in yesterday about mid-day, to announce Marshal Soult's submission (I believe) to the new order of things, and to arrange cantonments, &c., for the two armies.   He was closeted with General Murray a long time, and arrangements were made.   He returned this morning to have the articles ratified, and to-night Lord G. Lennox has orders to be in readiness to go to England through Paris with the news.   This last fact you will perhaps have heard, and probably before you get this.

We had yesterday our grand *Te Deum,* a most strange noisy military and religious ceremony attended with all the drums and military bands; French civic soldiers, with their hats on, hallooing, shouting, singing, organs, &c., an immense crowd, and great cordiality. Unluckily, Gazan passed the door as the crowd was coming out ; he was hooted, and saluted with *" A bas Soult,"* &c. This was a pity, but these changeable gentlemen are all in extremes. The troops are all going into cantonments immediately, and we shall for some time, I conclude, be quiet.

The bad news from Bayonne is very unlucky. General Hope is, I hear, not dangerously wounded, and his aid-de-camp is gone to Bayonne to comfort him in his confinement, which I trust will now be soon over. His affair seems to have been a surprise in a great measure, and the chief loss was in regaining the church, &c., of St. Etienne, which had been easily lost at first. Lord Dalhousie, on the other hand, seems to have gone on well alone, across the Dordogne.

The arsenal is here on a very large scale, and would have been a very great acquisition, were the war to have gone on. The French carried away almost everything but materials, of which there is abundance of wheels, carriages, &c., and all the forges, &c., in order.

Head-Quarters, Toulouse, April 23rd, 1814.—Our life now has fallen into the old routine way again,

and not only without daily events and little incidents to excite the mind as has hitherto been the
case, but also with the additional flatness and indifference, which cannot but be felt so immediately
after a succession of such occurrences as have taken
place within the last month. You will now have
only the tittle-tattle of a country town (a French
one certainly, and therefore somewhat novel), and
you must be satisfied. When Count Gazan came
over here, to settle the terms of armistice and
line of demarkation, &c., with Generals Murray and
Wimpfen, he was so much engaged that I could
not see him as I wished to do, and he went very
suddenly back again. The terms I conclude you
will see in the papers.

When the Spanish garrisons are collected in
France, this southern French army will again be
respectable. Our troops are all moving into their
cantonments along the Garonne on the left bank,
excepting a few on this right bank, within the department of the Haute Garonne, which remains
nearly all ours for the present. We have had a
variety of strangers—the two Sir Charles Stewarts
in the first place. The Lisbon minister only stopped
here one day on his way to Holland, the other Sir

Charles from Paris came, as it is whispered here, to signify a wish on the part of the Allies that Lord Wellington would be the English commissioner at the general Congress; if so, and it seems very probable, I think he does well to refuse, as he cannot stand higher than he does. Were he to go, the other diplomatists would be surprised at his method of getting through business. We should certainly have a general peace many weeks sooner, if not months, than we are likely to have otherwise.

I was walking with C—— in Lord Wellington's garden about eight o'clock in the morning, three days since, when we saw a queer-looking figure approach, of whom we could make out nothing from the complete mixture of undress and magnificence— a pair of not clean overalls on, a common short pelisse, and a foraging cap, but the whole breast covered with stars and little crosses, and swords and orders of all sorts.

I was not a little surprised at being introduced to Sir C. Stewart. He had arrived at two in the morning and had gone to bed, without sending word to Lord Wellington, depending upon finding him at home at eight o'clock, when to his mortification he found Lord Wellington had been since five in the morning out hunting; and when Sir C. asked where he could go to meet him, the best information he could get was, that it was in a forest somewhere about eighteen miles distant, but no one knew exactly where, as the only persons who knew, about four in number, were out with him. Patience, therefore, was his only remedy, and instead of being off again in two hours as he said he had intended, he was obliged to stay long enough to give us a few anecdotes from the Allies. Two of Marshal Suchet's aides-de-camp, and two or three French colonels from his army and Soult's, have also been here.

One of Suchet's I had much conversation with— a gentleman-like young man. He told me Suchet was at Perpignan when he heard of Soult's affair here; but, that he then thought it prudent to hasten to Narbonne, and there he was when the Paris news arrived. Had the war gone on, therefore, we should evidently have had a dance as I expected, to the Mediterranean on the road to Montpelier after these united marshals, and should have required your utmost exertions and reinforcements from England; as it is, all is well. Suchet's aide-de-camp said he found very different feelings towards Soult in this country, from what there were towards his master in the districts where he had commanded, that he feared Soult had conducted himself very badly. The two marshals are, I understand, very jealous of each other. I asked him if Suchet had the least notion, or expectation previously of what has happened, he said, " No; who could expect such a change in the minds of every one, and such a revolution in seven days' time ?" Then he laughed, and said, " At present we were *à la mode ;*" and as I met him at the grand ball at the Capitole here again, he said, " There, you have nothing to do now but to make the most of your advantages, and amuse yourselves ; all the beauties have now declared for you."

I rather pitied him, when at that meeting, a number of pert apprentices with immense white cockades on, and some still with Napoleon buttons, and smart civic uniforms, were continually coming up to him and reaching about up to his chin, asking him pertly, " Oh! are you Soult's aide-de-camp, or Suchet's ? well how do you like what is going on ?"—fellows that a month ago would have almost cleaned his shoes had they been asked. Some of them even thought he was English, and in bad patois

French, complimented him on the progress he had made in the French language. His military pride was much put to the trial, and he could hardly smother his feelings. He then asked me, to show him his new King, of whom there was an old picture hung up, as he said it was now time to make acquaintance with his new sovereign, as well as with this new state of society.

The grand ball given by the town at the Capitole on Thursday went off well, except that it was just such a crowd as an Easter Monday ball at the Mansion House. The rooms were very handsome, and the five hundred English, Spanish, and Portuguese officers added not a little to the appearance of the scene. Nearly the whole were generals, aide-de-camps, staff-officers, or at least field-officers, and every order and ornament of every nation was worn. Lord Wellington was most splendid. The amusement commenced by leading him into the Salle de Trone *ci-devant* Bonaparte, where, over the vacant chair, in the centre, was the picture of King Louis XVIII., and on each side that of the Duc d'Angoulême, and one of Lord Wellington himself —the latter a hasty caricature likeness taken by a painter here at the play from memory. He was then entertained with a short concert, principally consisting of " La Chasse d'Henri IV.," and " God save the King," sung by the public singers from a gallery, amidst the clouds, goddesses and cupids painted above them.

I had got Mr. K——, the famous English officer singer, to go with me to the leader of the band, and to give him the catch-club harmony of " God save the King," and we wrote them down full instructions, and all the words for the song, solo, trio, chorus, &c., &c., the words spelt also in the French pronunciation, while the musician caught by the ear and scribbled down all the parts, one by one, from K——'s singing. It was an entertaining scene. They had a rehearsal, and Mr. K—— gave the *prima donna* a few private lessons, and the whole, in consequence, went off really surprisingly well. The supper-tables were filled by about four sets successively, the English having the preference, sentinels letting us in, and keeping out the French until the last. This went on until there was not even bread and water remaining.

The press, now, is at work here, printing Cevallo's old history of the conduct of the French in Spain, and a variety of things, which, to the

natives, are news. There seems to be a disposition
to buy the books and read; nothing, however, will
make the French what Cobbett calls us "a thinking people." They seem to be as frivolous as ever.
The next thing wished for here and at Bordeaux,
is, now, to get rid of this new constitution, and
have the Bourbons as before : at least the party is
strong for this line, and, unless something decisive
is done soon, and the old military dispersed about,
and gens-d'armes, I think they will even yet have
a squabble about several things, among themselves,
which makes me wish that we should be off as
soon as possible, and have nothing to do with
them. As soon as all the foreign garrisons are withdrawn, and the line of the French empire settled,
the faster we withdraw from within it the better.
I always expected the royal cause would gain
ground as it has, when once fairly tried. It was
the only source of peace, and that was what all
wanted, on any terms. Of course the acceptance of
the Bourbons made it all easy; but, I believe, all
the southern departments would gladly have been
English, to secure peace, and get sugar, sell their
wines, and get rid of conscriptions and acquisitions.

Lord Wellington gives another grand ball at the

ci-devant Prefecture, now Palais Royal, on Monday next. On Tuesday, he resigns his place there to the Duc d'Angoulême, and as there is an old adage about two kings of Brentford, I suspect he will soon afterwards take a trip somewhere else, at least for a time. I doubt, however, his leaving the armies altogether, while they remain in force, and the French marshals likewise.

Bordeaux must be very proud of the example they have given to France. They must take especial care to conceal their subsequent alarms, and half repentance of what they have done.

CHAPTER VI.

TOULOUSE—ITS CHURCHES—PROTESTANT SERVICE—LIBRARIES
— RECEPTION OF THE DUC D'ANGOULEME — THE FRENCH
GENERALS—POPULARITY OF WELLINGTON.

Head-Quarters, Toulouse,
April 27, 1814.

MY DEAR M——

THOUGH I have nothing now to amuse you
with, but the result of my morning walks and
inquiries in this town, I shall proceed as usual,
more with a wish to preserve my own crude observations, than hoping to interest you much by the
perusal.

My last was finished on Saturday. On Sunday,
about half-past eleven, I attended the service at
the Protestant Chapel, established under the
sanction and patronage of Bonaparte, as a sort of
church-wardenish gold-lettered record informed
me. The service began with a prayer by the clerk;

he then gave out a psalm, more noisy than musical, and without the accompaniment of the organ. I was only astonished that such a small congregation could make so much noise and discord. One greasy-headed, methodistical-looking man, near me, continued in an unceasing roar, bearing much more resemblance to a well-known noise, with which our mules so frequently indulge us, than any known harmony. A short prayer, and a long chapter from the New Testament, with the Commentary, as printed in the book, was then delivered from the pulpit or reading-desk (as there was but one) by a clergyman, who then entered. Another Psalm ensued. The organ then played, to introduce a young preacher, who took the reader's place, and gave us a prayer and the Ten Commandments, and another psalm, partly to the organ; but before half a stave was finished, the organist found that his notes and the vocal ones were so different, that he ceased playing, and though he made two or three attempts at a single note afterwards, he found it would not do, and gave it up.

The young preacher then read a text from the Bible, and gave us a very good extempore dis- course about half-an-hour long. The subject was the vanity of this world, and the danger of temptation and evil communication. The language and delivery were clear and distinct; there was no rant, but much propriety of manner. A psalm followed, and the organ was not so much distanced; then the Lord's Prayer and Belief, and a prayer for all descriptions of persons and denominations, like that of our own Church praying for dignitaries, &c. And then another psalm, at last, in tolerable harmony, but very noisy. A blessing concluded the whole.

At first, there was only about forty-five persons; some half-dozen old gentlemen were in the seats near the altar. These had backs. About twenty-five women were in the right-hand seats; and about fifteen men in the left. The side seats were chairs placed in rows, and all fastened to each other. In the course of the service, the numbers increased to about sixty or seventy. The congregation appeared to be all (nearly) of the middling class of tradesmen; only about three of our poor men took their allotted seats quite at the back. As no one ever knelt down, there was no occasion for either room or cushions for that purpose. The men sat with their hats occasionally on and off, and legs crossed, at their ease, in the style of the House of Commons; but were attentive to the sermon. The three poor men all fell asleep, snoring so loud, that a sort of beadle was obliged to awaken them. I was not much surprised on the whole, comparing this scene with that in the Roman Catholic churches, that the proselytes amongst the highest and lower classes were not numerous. This service suits neither. It is most adapted to an independent tradesman, who thinks a little for himself, and can see the errors of the Catholics, and likes the economy of the chapel. It might be accident, but I saw scarcely any white cockades,— only one or two of the elder, and I suppose richer members of the community wear them in their hats.

On Monday I looked into nearly all the churches, present and *ci-devant,* of Toulouse. The cathedral St. Etienne, I have already mentioned. The next in size and consequence is St. Saturnin, or more commonly called St. Surnin. This is a curious building, in the dark heavy Saxon style (reminding one of the early attempts at Grecian revival, and the introduction of the Gothic), all circular except the angular main pillars of the centre of the cross, which were heavy octagons; the roof circular, and upper windows double circles. Except the pillars, nearly the whole is made of the flat tile or brick, which is curious. It was built in the present form about the year 1160 to 1190. There are monuments of the Earls of Toulouse, &c., of founders, and in a dark vaulted chapel under the grand altar, are relics innumerable—of the thorns in the crown placed on the head of Christ; the heads of Barnabas, of Simon, and of Jude; parts of their bodies also; parts of Peter; besides bishops, &c.; the body and figure of Thomas Aquinas; and an English saint, a king, whose name I could not make out. We heard much of the riches with which all these relics were formerly surrounded. It is said the revolutionists carried off four hundredweight of gold, besides silver. All the most valuable part, however, as the good Catholics are bound to think, were fortunately spared, and still remain in excellent preservation, and tolerably fine with gilding.

The general effect of the building is gloomy and superstitious, and a strange unpleasant smell, which some say proceeds from large vaults underneath, which are filled with bodies which do not

corrupt, makes one glad to get out of the building
as soon as curiosity is satisfied.   They do not bury
their dead in the church now, and the vaults I mentioned are walled up.   In the remaining churches
now in use there is little worthy of notice, but
there are two very large *ci-devaut* convent
churches.   That of the Jacobins is curious; one long
building only, like King's College Chapel (not a
cross), and with one lofty row of circular pillars
all down the centre.   This forms as it were two
equal main aisles, and no side aisles.   On the sides
are rows of chapels and a large cloister.   The
whole almost is in brick, except the centre pillars.
It is now regularly fitted up as a cavalry barrack
stables, and they are excellent, easily containing
in the whole, I should think, about seven hundred
horses.   There is an octagon building adjoining,
with a slender pillar, fitted up the same.   Near this
is another large, long, similar building, formerly a
chapel, but without the centre pillars, and the
scale somewhat smaller, of course.   This is the
forage store for the cavalry barrack.   We have
them now both in use as the French had.   I must
now be off in my best to meet the Duc d'Angoulême.

Friday, the 29*th.*—About two o'clock on Wednesday the most interesting scene since that of the first day, and a more splendid one, commenced. Lord Wellington, surrounded by about three hundred horsemen, composed of general officers, aides-de-camp, and staff-officers of all descriptions, and of the four nations, Spanish, English, French, and Portuguese, went out to meet the Duc d'Angoulême, all in the best uniforms, on the best chargers, and covered with white cockades. The only French general of our opposing army who came in time for this was Clausel, and he was for some time side by side with Lord Wellington. When we had gone about six miles, and arrived at a sort of triumphal arch on a hill, the Duke appeared, escorted by a guard of our heavy dragoons and a double French guard of honour from Bordeaux and Toulouse. We drew up at each side, after the interview with Lord Wellington, to let them pass, and then all joined in the procession to the town.

The sides of the road were crowded with carriages and people, and the enthusiasm of the lower classes, and of the women in particular, was excessive. The Duke and Lord Wellington, after being joined by more guards of honour and more suite, as we approached the town, entered the streets over the grand bridge, amidst the shouts and acclamations of a multitude crowding every window. The scene reminded me of the London streets at Lord Nelson's funeral. From the *tête de pont*, which still in part exists, over the bridge, up to the cathedral through all the principal streets, was a double line of English troops, between which the procession passed. Several of the regiments had got their clothing, and they looked admirably, especially the Scotch 91st.

A sort of moveable *garde urbaine de l'infanterie* on each side kept also with us all the way. White flags, exhibiting French ingenuity to the utmost, were hanging from every window. Sheets, table-cloths, towels, &c., covered with green paper fleurs-de-lys, formed excellent standards, and paper flags were innumerable. The women, and some of the old men, were quite mad with joy, and screamed, *Vive le Roi et vivent les Anglais!* till they were stopped by absolute exhaustion, or some by tears of joy. Every house was hung with laurel mixed with the white, and the lower story covered entirely with old tapestry, old carpets or sheets, and paper fleurs-de-lys. In the morning this made the streets look something like Broker's-alley certainly, but the effect, when mixed with the rest of the scene, was not bad.

After passing under another triumphal arch of table-cloths, laurel, fleurs-de-lys, &c., we reached the cathedral, and a *Te Deum* succeeded. This was much like the last, only rather more in order, and the public bodies were more numerous and in their costume. The ten Judges and the President, in their red robes, like our aldermen, with small black-and-gold caps. The Judges de Premier Instance, in black Master-of-Arts gowns, with sky-blue sashes ; the Avocats in black gowns alone ; the professors of sciences and arts in their crimson-coloured Master-of-Arts gowns, and those of belles-lettres in orange ; the Archbishop and clergy in full costume, &c. The music was not very striking, but many of the old people cried with joy.

About six o'clock the Duke dined with Lord Wellington, and went to the play in the evening, where the acclamations were renewed with fresh vigour ; the women in the streets caught hold of his coat to kiss it. Yesterday the Duke had a *grande messe*, and then a full-dress drawing-room—

this in the morning. In the evening the great
rooms of the Capitolium were opened again for
music and dancing. The Duke came in there too
soon, when scarcely five hundred people were arrived, but in another hour the crowd was immense.
The dresses of the women were very splendid, and
the variety of orders and uniforms made the scene
very gay. General Villette was there, as well as
Clausel, and a number of French officers. The
Duke was just the same as at St. Jean de Luz, and
remembered all his old acquaintance there, myself
among the rest.

He not only gave me a gracious nod during the
first procession, but surprised me by coming round
behind the chairs of the ladies, where I was standing, in the music-room, and gave me his hand, and
reminded me of the King Joseph's saddle-cloth,
which I had given the Duke, and which was on his
horse, as I observed, when he entered the town.
His affability and good nature are striking; but he
must acquire more dignity and self-possession, as
his figure is against him in appearance, and he
seems shy; in short, he must learn the trade of
Kingcraft, like any other, and a quiet rational man
is just now the best King the French can have.

The great rock to avoid is the probability of being misled by indiscreet emigrants.

I was, I must own, rather at a loss myself what to say to the Duke, but when he talked of the saddle-cloth, I replied, "Its only merit, which was as a trophy, now was at an end, as the family of the Bonapartes had ceased to be objects to triumph over." This, and a lame congratulation on what had happened, completed my speech; as, however, it was as new to me to address royalty as it was to him to act it, I hope if occasion offers I may improve by practice as well as his Highness. One thing has amused me much in all this scene; the good city of Toulouse covered its streets with sand, and made the air resound with its cries, and every house had two paper lanterns in every window at night; and they were in general, I am convinced, sincere in this, although one might have been induced to think otherwise from the acts of the authorities and public officers. A set of garde urbain officers (the new gens-d'armes), ran all the way at the head of the processions, prompting the cries, and setting them going all the way we went, and the illuminations were by special order of the mayor from the Bureau d'Illuminations, as usual

in the time of Bonaparte's system.   My intended
observation is this—the city loyalty vented itself in
cries, in *Te Deums,* in music, and in farthing candles, and dancing, shouting, draperies, &c., but the
Royal Duke was placed in the Palais Royal (*ci-
devant* Prefecture), and no provision made for his
table or for his establisment or Bordeaux guard of
honour, and our head-quarters Commissary was
called upon to feed the animals, &c., of the guard
and followers, and Lord Wellington to entertain
the Prince and invite the principal citizens to meet
him.

The old notion of the sign of the Four Alls—
"John Bull pays for all," seems to be as well
known here as elsewhere in the world.   There
seems no principle now-a-days more generally dif-
fused or adopted more readily in every quarter.
Our rations are all procured, you must be aware,
by requisitions, through the mayors of the country,
&c., to be provided by the districts, and you would
naturally think the same authority could provide
for all French deserters, and for the Royal troops
of guards and establishment; but then who would
pay for all these requisitions?   All we have is paid
for, and it is *bien plus commode* to come to our

store ready collected than to form one for these purposes.

An odd incident occurred to me just before the procession on Wednesday. I was at Lord Wellington's new hotel, the great inn, the Hotel de France, endeavouring to find his room, to leave a Court-martial, when I stumbled on my friend the Dutch aide-de-camp of General Clausel, who told me he was looking for one of our Marshal's aides-de-camp in waiting, to introduce his General, who was behind him, and who, on my turning round, recognized me, as he and his division took me prisoner. To their great surprise, I told them there was no chance of finding an aide-de-camp, but perhaps we might find a sergeant, and I was on the search. It so happened there was no one but an ignorant sentinel. In trying a door or two, we all blundered upon Lord Wellington, who came himself to the door, so I introduced the astonished Clausel and walked off.

My Dutch friend told me that Soult and Suchet would have had about six aides-de-camp, &c., in the first room, and a General officer in waiting in the second. I own I think our great man is in the opposite extreme, but he does not

like being watched and plagued. Just after the
state *levée* yesterday, I saw him cross the crowded
square in his blue coat and round hat, almost un-
noticed and unknown even to the very people who
half an hour before had been cheering him. In one
angle of Lord Wellington's hotel lives Madame
C——, a Spanish beauty, married into a French
family of rank, who are the proprietors of the
hotel, but who have been obliged to let nearly the
whole, reserving this angle. I do not mean to be
scandalous, but this perhaps may have decided the
choice of the house.

Lord Wellington to-day had intelligence that
Marshal Suchet was on his way here, and has been
with his staff about a dozen miles to meet him in
form. The French Marshal, from some confusion,
did not appear, and Lord Wellington would wait
no longer, but returned alone. In our grand procession to meet the royal Duke on Wednesday a
ridiculous accident happened. A French post
carriage with three horses abreast ran away and
came full drive down upon us, the Frenchmen
all bawling, the horses pulling all ways and clearing all before them. Our three hundred warriors
were all broken in an instant and dispersed over

the ditches, and in all directions, until at last one unfortunate horseman ran foul of the French horses, and the whole came down together. Fortunately, nobody was materially hurt.

Saturday, Post-day.—As I returned home last night by the Palais Royal from dinner, I found every one going without regular invitation into the Palais Royal to the Prince, who held a *soirée;* so I entered likewise, and found him surrounded by dancing as usual, and by Marshals and Generals only to be outdone at Paris. Suchet had arrived with his staff. Colonel Canning, who was left behind for him, brought him in about two hours after Lord Wellington returned. General Lamarque and several other officers came with him, two Generals as aides-de-camp, besides Colonels, &c. The Marshal himself was a strange figure. His head and cheeks and chin all overgrown with hair, like a wild man of the woods; and his dress more splendid than the drum-major of one of our Guards' bands on a birthday.

The contrast had a singular effect. The uniform was blue, but almost concealed, and could have stood alone with gold embroidery. Every seam, edge, and button, before and behind, above and below, was *gallone* with a sort of oak-leaf pattern, about three inches wide, and on his breast were two gold and silver stars, as large as our Garter star, and several small orders of different kinds. He would have been rather a good-looking man if dressed in a more moderate style. Lord Wellington and several of his Generals, being in their plain uniform, made the French General's extravagance the more striking.

Soult's aide-de-camp also came in, and a guard was ready, and an hotel for him, but he did not appear. Generals Lamarque, Clausel, Villette, and three or four more, and a number of embroidered *Payeurs* and *Commissaires Généraux, Préfets,* &c., increased the general glitter; but nothing looked better than our scarlet. The Prince and Suchet had much conversation, and seemed more easy and gay, than I had seen the former before with any of his new friends.

Scarcely any Frenchman has worn the Spanish or Portuguese cockade, and amidst all the cries you never hear a *viva* for either Spaniards or Portuguese. They are in consequence very angry and sulky, and I think a little jealous of us. This you may well imagine, when you learn that they all along consider that *they* have accomplished all that has happened, and that we have assisted a little certainly, but that they could have done without us. Except those about Lord Wellington, who do it more out of compliment to him, the Spaniards in general, and a great number of the Portuguese, will not in consequence wear the white cockade.

I see no harm in this, for as we fought a whole century to prevent the two kingdoms of France and Spain from being both under the Bourbons, it is quite as well now that it happens to be our interest to fight for the contrary doctrine, that there should be as little cordiality between them as possible. A Spanish soldier was told the other day in the street to cry " *Vive le Roi! Vivent les Bourbons.*" He made no answer. The request was repeated, and he was asked why he made a difficulty. He was still silent at first, but then rapped out a favourite Spanish oath, then " *Viva Fernando VII.! Viva Lord Wellington!* Los Espanioles care for nothing more;" and nothing more would he say.

It is remarkable enough, but the fact is, that Lord Wellington is very popular with the common

Spanish soldiers, I am told, and with the country people; but with the generality of officers, regimental in particular, and with the highest classes in Spain, it is rather the reverse.

It is curious now to see Lord Wellington play the second fiddle, having been so long established leader. It will serve to break him in by degrees for England and peace. He carries it off very well. Most of our Lieutenant-Generals are gone to Paris, or going, and many other officers. I suppose I shall do best by remaining with the army to the last, or at least as long as Lord Wellington remains, and then going straight to London and reporting my arrival.

At the Capitolium on Thursday, young B——, with whom I was talking, as we were very hot and tired, persuaded me to sit down with him on the bottom step of the vacant throne. The Prince and all the grandees were then in another room, but we were soon routed up by the garde urbaine sentinel, to the mortification and vexation of my young honourable companion at not being allowed at Toulouse what he was entitled to in the House of Lords in England. He is well—dancing away cotillions, waltzes, &c.

Later.—We have just had an arrival, and Lord Wellington quits this for Paris immediately; I hope, however, that he will return shortly, as he now intends to do.   We all here said that matters would never be well arranged at Paris without him, and that he would go at last.

Head-Quarters, Toulouse, May 2nd, 1814.— Having thanked you for your letter of the 12th of April, and papers to the same date, I must proceed on my old subject, Toulouse, and its sights and curiosities, regretting, on your account, as well as my own, that they are not more interesting.

The great cannon-foundry was formerly one of the most prominent, but it has now ceased to work for nearly three or four years.   How or why this could happen, when military works and manufactures seemed alone to flourish in France during that period, I cannot say.   The fact is, everything remains in a state as if the workmen were only all gone away to dinner, but in silent desolation, like a scene in Herculaneum, or Southey's town under water.   Unfinished moulds, guns, &c., and tools are lying about in all directions.   To show how much the whole has been neglected, even *Egalité* has been suffered to remain on one entrance pillar, *Liberté* on the other, and the word *Impériale* in the middle. The fleur-de-lys will, I suppose, find its way there soon by some accident.

Suchet now commands both armies here. He told the Duc d'Angoulême he had sixteen thousand men of his own army at his service. This hero, to whom the day of the month, yesterday (May-day), reminded me of a much nearer resemblance than the drum-major, has left us, and is off to his troops.

There are two public libraries here, in which I have spent the better part of a morning each, one containing about thirty thousand volumes, the other about twenty-five thousand. The former has too large a proportion of ecclesiastical learning; but they both contain some good editions of classics and good historians, annals, &c., particularly the smaller library. They are old episcopal and private foundations, and have neither gained nor lost much by the Revolution, which is rather curious. There seems to have been no very valuable early editions or manuscripts—nothing very much worth plundering; and they say they were too conscientious to take advantage of the times, and enrich themselves by plunder. The arrangement of the books is not bad. Firstly, good polyglot and other Bibles of all kinds; then commentaries on sacred history, &c.; then history in general; then laws of nations, &c.; then laws in general, essays, &c.; then French voyages, arts, sciences, classics, and belles-lettres. There is an atlas of the Grand Canal and its vicinity on an immense scale, which might have been important had we proceeded, though I think no other stand would have been made until after we had gone beyond the limits of the canal, and after a junction of Soult with Suchet at Narbonne. Amongst the books pointed out as of the most interest, were Racine's Greek editions of Euripides and Æschylus, containing his name and several notes in his own handwriting,—a remarkably neat hand. The editions were Stephens' and Stanley's. The notes were either short free translations of passages and sentiments, or memoranda to call attention to particular passages for future use and application, or they were short remarks of approbation or disapprobation of scenes, passages, &c. I copied out nearly the whole, not being very long, and I enclose them. I shall thank you to put them into my Euripides or somewhere, to be preserved.

Several of the private houses here of the merchants and nobles are on a very large scale, and
contain very spacious suites of rooms round the
court-yard. The architecture is, in general, very
moderate. Most of the mansions have only the
merit of extent, and one or two of which have an
attempt at more are in bad taste. The one most
remarkable is particularly so. It has an immense
heavy stone cornice, out of all proportion, and the
capitals of all the pillars are a species of false
Corinthian, or rather, Composite, with the upper
ornaments, spread eagles, in most barbarous taste,
and in the place of the most beautiful part of the
true pillars of the Composite order.

Toulouse appears, in size, to have been for a
very considerable time, nearly stationary. There
is not, as in some of our country towns, and some
in France, the new town as well as the old. The
old brick walls, with occasional towers, remain
entire nearly all round, and still form nearly the
city boundary, as there is scarcely any suburbs
without the walls; at several of the entrances
within there seems to have been some vacant
spaces, and in two or three places an ornamental
sort of crescent or square has been commenced,—

one lately, but the others before the Revolution.
They are all unfinished. In general, however, all
within the city walls is covered with building of
some sort or another.

The splendid façade of the Capitolium was
raised before the Revolution. Henry IV. commenced the work, it is said, and his statue remains there. A very small beginning has been
made towards stone façades on one of the other
sides of the Grande Place of the Capitol, but in
general the old shabby buildings still remain, and
seem likely to do so, for some time to come.

May 3rd.—Our prince is gone to review his new
army under Suchet, and leaves us quiet. Every
day carries off some of our higher officers, and we
all expect to move the instant Lord Wellington
returns, if not before. To-morrow, if possible, I go
with a party and passport to see the great basin De
Feriol, the main feeder of the Grand Canal. It is
the sight of this country, and therefore, though I
expect to be disappointed, I have agreed to join
Dr. Macgregor and a party to-morrow, and return
the next day. It is about thirty-two miles off,
near Revel.

I yesterday attended the Court of Appeal here

for the four departments around—Aude, Tarn, Lot
and Garonne, and Arriège.   There were ten judges
present: there exist, and may be present as many
as sixteen, and a quorum of seven is necessary
to form a Court.   There were, besides the *Pro-
cureur-Général* and *Avocat-Général*, about twenty-
five barristers in gowns, nearly like ours, but with
bonnets instead of wigs.   They were dirty, and
mostly old, and looked precisely like a set of
provincial barristers in England.   The same habits
make the manners and appearance so similar in
nations nearly equally civilized, that, until the language betrayed the difference, I could have fancied
myself in England again.

The subject in dispute was half an acre of vine-
yard, and it turned on the construction of a
confused legacy in a will of an old gentleman.   The
eagerness with which the contest was maintained
reminded me of a Court of Quarter Sessions in
England,—all talking at once and with abundance
of noise and action, especially just as the ten
judges, like our juries, had laid their heads
together to consider, and whilst *le Procureur-
Général* was summing up the law and argument
previously to the Court.   Either the lawyers and

judges must be starving, or the judicial establishment must be very expensive in France now.

There are, besides this Court, others of *Premier Instance* in each department, and in four departments you have more judges than in England. Unless some changes are made, I think the French will find their whole government, which is calculated for a larger empire, in every way much too expensive. This will prevent any great reduction of ordinary taxation. The King and his court to be paid; the senate; all the marshals and grand dignitaries, the prefêts, &c. Each department now has a salary to pay its prefêt, nearly as large as that of an intendant of a whole province before the Revolution. The King will find abundance of patronage if this goes on; but a great part of the national income will be consumed in the management and support of the different species of rulers. One advantage in this, I hope, will be to keep France more quiet in future, as I have otherwise little faith in the present temper of this changeable race.

May 7, 1814. Post-day.—At five o'clock on Wednesday morning I went to Dr. Macgregor's to breakfast, preparatory to our expedition to St.

Feriol, as we had obtained our leave and a passport for that purpose. Our party consisted of Dr.
H——, Colonel G——, and P——, General H——,
and Mr. J——, and Mrs. J——. On account of
the latter, who was in an interesting condition, we
set out on the canal road towards Castelnaudary,
that she might go in the boat. We rode along the
towing path very pleasantly for about twenty miles.
Finding that Castelnaudary would be so much out
of the way, we then left the canal and rode across
through Villefranche and St. Felix to Revel, about
twenty-two miles further. This water scheme
delayed us much, so that we did not reach Revel
until seven or eight at night, and it also lengthened
our ride considerably.

The ordinary dinner at twelve, at the lock-house,
was, however, entertaining, and made up for this
in part, but, in truth, ladies should learn on these
occasions, when in such a state, to stay at home.
We expected a *malheur* every hour, she was so
fatigued.

On Thursday morning, after breakfast, we went
three miles to Sorege, to see the great college or
school establishment there, which is about three
miles from Revel. It was formerly attached to a

convent, and a sort of government military establishment. At the Revolution the buildings were
sold, and the present director and his brother, who
was one of the professors of the old establishment,
bought the whole, and undertook to continue, and,
as they say, to improve the plan as a private speculation. There are now about three hundred
boys, from eight to nineteen, or even twenty-one
years old. On the present arrangement, four
hundred and forty is the limit. I am told the
number once amounted to nearly six or seven hundred. There are now about thirty Protestant boys,
the rest are Catholics. Most of the Spanish boys,
once very numerous, left the school during the late
war. This peace, it is supposed, will bring them
back, even in greater numbers. English boys are
also expected to come again, as formerly.

The building is very spacious, and is prettily
situated, under the side of a mountainous tract of
country, at the head of a valley. The accommodation is very ample, and the order and arrangement very great, though, I think, it is less cleanly
than the college at Aire. The studies are more
varied, and the whole is complete in itself, as there
is a priest, a doctor, an Italian professor of mine-

ralogy, anatomy, a riding-master, and teachers of all kinds. The regular studies for all the boys are French, Latin, a little Greek, mathematics to some extent, dancing, swimming, drawing from models and casts, perspective, drawing from anatomical study, fortification, &c.; and for the upper boys riding—for which purpose about sixteen horses are at the disposal of the riding-master. In addition to this every boy has his own bedstead of iron, and all the two upper classes, of the three into which the whole school is divided, have separate places to sleep in. Every boy, at a certain time, either follows in his studies the choice of his parents, or his own inclination, and may learn Italian, German, English, Spanish, or any musical instrument; even the pianoforte. The drawing-school is hung round with the approved productions of the boys, and is spacious, and so is the riding-school. There is also a theatre, regularly fitted up, in which the boys recite, and act plays and perform concerts; asking the neighbours to come and form an audience. The establishment also contains a small botanical garden, a tolerable collection of mineralogy, and a piece of water for the purpose of swimming. The boys were all in uniform, and looked healthy and well. As they come from all quarters, it is usual to leave them there all the year round, and this is rather expected and desired. They come clothed at first, but afterwards everything is found them, and the parents have nothing to do but to pay *mille francs*, about 45*l*. or 50*l*., annually, and no bills or extras of any kind are ever sent or charged, whatever may be learnt by the boys : this is rather dearer than at Aire or St Sever, I believe, but not much, when all circumstances are considered.

We found the schoolmasters consequential and prosy, as they usually are with us. The Italian, who was more particularly so, was formerly the professor who managed the Grand Duke of Tuscany's collection. This education would, I think, suit many an orphan or natural son destined for the English army, and with small means. He would join his regiment at eighteen, with much more useful knowledge than could be obtained for the same money in England, as to languages, &c., and much information useful to a military man. He would also come away with, at least, one or two accomplishments probably, by which he might amuse himself in country quarters, and be kept out of mischief. It might also answer for mercantile men, merchants, clerks, &c., though perhaps some of these pursuits would only make them idle. Most of the boys are destined for merchants or soldiers, as I understood. For other professions I think we have as good, or better, and as cheap an education in Yorkshire, and other places in England. This sort of education accounts for the general distribution of a certain extent of acquirement which we see amongst the French officers, and for the advantages they possess as to the power of self-amusement. When prisoners of war, they have a smattering of drawing, dancing, singing, music, acting, &c.

We then went to the basin of St. Feriol. On our way I rode up a valley to see some foundries of copper, which were much talked of; only one of a number was at work, as times were so bad. I found the copper was Swedish, and only worked there on account of the facilities of wood and water to work the bellows and anvil. The work in which the men were then engaged, was making saucepans and pots, and stewing-pans, for the Toulouse ships, and on a very small scale. I always like to ascertain that there is nothing to see when a sight is talked of. We went then over the hill to the basin.

I must own I was rather surprised with the extent of this, and though it was almost exactly what I expected to find it, I was very glad I had come over to see it. The shape of the ground, and course of the stream, were particularly fortunate and well adapted to the plan, and the great dam or dike, which pens back the water, so as to form a small lake, in depth near the wall from fifty to sixty feet, is a noble work. It consists of three main walls, well *terrassed* or puddled between each, and with two large arched vaults, one quite at the bottom, covering the natural bed of the river; the other higher up, and leading to the *robinets* or great cocks, which let out the water as required. The river coming down the valley fills the basin, not being able to find its vent, and therefore spreading over the ground, and filling all the hollows up to the dam wall, which is about sixty feet high. The banks, except the natural dam, are the natural shape of the ground, and there is no excavation at all; when full the water, as required, is let out by a hatch, and so runs by into the stream, which conducts it, after about ten miles circuit, to the highest point of the canal, from whence the locks descend both ways to Toulouse, and to the Mediterranean. It then sup-

plies both. When the basin is low, the next opening is a sort of hatch or floodgate, lower down in
the wall; when lower still the water is let off by
three great *robinets* or cocks at the end of the
voûte, about thirty feet or so below the surface.
When these are opened, the rushing of the water
makes a tremendous noise, at a distance like
thunder. When it is required to empty or clean
the basin, &c. the river is turned off, and the contents of the basin empty themselves in the original
bed of the stream : the contents of the basin are, I
think, six millions of tons of water. There is
another smaller basin, about ten miles higher up,
in the mountains, and another near the canal,
whence the stream enters it.

The whole seems well managed. The canal itself is kept in great order, like our New River,
the banks trimmed, &c., and in width it exceeds
even our Royal Canal in Ireland, by several yards,
I should think.

With much delay and difficulty, we got Mrs. J——
through these sights, after much unnecessary alarm
and fright in the vaults. We returned about five
to dinner at Revel, where we slept again yesterday :
we had a hot ride home through Caraman and

Lentar, about thirty-two miles. The country round the canal, and in the bottoms, is rich and fertile, but contains little wood. It is like some of our Somersetshire and Dorsetshire valleys, but more covered with villas and chateaux, and villages. The road back, by Caraman, is through a much poorer country, but also like the higher bad parts of Somersetshire, and that neighbourhood — such as near Chard and the hills round Bath.

The villages seem in a decaying state, and the inhabitants poor, but the country, upon the whole, is in much better condition, in point of cultivation and appearance, than one could suppose, after what has passed in the last twenty years. In one or two out-of-the-way places we were stared at, and followed like monsters, or sights, but were everywhere well received by the people. At Sorege, some French cavalry was quartered, but they were nearly all gone to the grand review before the Duc d'Angoulême. I should like to have been there also, but we understood it would not be liked, and that the Duke was to go without English altogether; this was quite right. I am told that the review went off well, and that Soult himself set a good example.

It is strange to think of our carrying off Bona-parte in a frigate, and his conversation with Augereau is curious after the address of the latter to his men. King Joseph is gone off and escaped, but no one need be much afraid of him now.

The style of nearly all the French chateaux is similar; all front and appearance.

On my return yesterday I dined with Mr. B——and his French hosts, for I scarcely know whose dinner it was; I believe a joint effort. The wines were the patron's and very good. He is a man of fortune, a Monsieur de T——, and speaks English tolerably. The wife is a pleasing woman, and rather good-looking and young. They were very . civil, and she sang and played in the evening very fairly. At least she had much execution and dash if not feeling, in her playing. Like most of our young female players, she left out all the andantes and slow passages.

The furniture of the two or three rooms in which she lived was very splendid. Handsome carpets were alone wanting to make her own room in particular an elegant fine lady's drawing-room in England. In some respects, particularly as to the gilding, there was both more show and taste than generally are seen with us. The pianoforte was particularly handsome; it was by Erard of Paris, and though only a small one, cost a hundred Louis-d'or. The whole contents of her room cost, it is said, a thousand Louis-d'or.

In the variety and materials of the ladies' dresses here, there seems to be also a very considerable degree of luxury—more perhaps than with us.

We are now very dull, and as the Prince is still absent, do not even hear the " *Vive le Roi*," or "*Vivent les Bourbons*," &c., as usual. I was much amused yesterday at seeing posted up at a country inn, a halfpenny print of the royal Duc d'Angoulême in his best, on horseback, and surrounded by a copy of most loyal verses singing his praises and those of the Bourbons and the English, in the measure and going to the music of the famous Marseillais hymn; in short, a sort of parody of that song, beginning " *Allons enfans de la Garonne*," &c. What changes !

CHAPTER VII.

Head-Quarters, Toulouse,
May 11, 1814.

My dear M——,

THE very small number of sights which this town affords being exhausted, and Lord Wellington being still absent, we are in truth more dull than we should be in a country town in England. The only interesting subject of conversation now is, who goes to America, and who does not? Some of the regiments move to-day towards Bordeaux from hence for the purpose of embarking upon this new expedition, which I should think would all end in a mere demonstration. Lord Wellington is expected here to-morrow, and we shall then know what is to happen; and head-quarters will, I conclude, move immediately.

I have heard nothing since my last, and seen but one thing worth mentioning, and that is, Mr. Macarthy's library, which the old father and grandfather have been sixty years collecting, and which is now to be sold on the father's death for the benefit of the widow and nine children. This is the library for which the Duke of Devonshire offered 25,000*l.* sterling as it stands; but the bargain was never closed, as he wished the whole to be embarked at the risk of the owner, and they wanted to have the money for it as it stands here, to be moved by the purchaser. The owners now talk of sending it to Paris, and having a public sale there by auction, thinking that emperors and kings will then bid against the Duke of Devonshire, Earl Spencer, and others of our book-loving nobles.

It contains a considerable number of fine copies of " Principes editiones," filling one side of a large room, all upon vellum. There is also Cardinal Ximenes' polyglot edition of the Bible; his own copy—the only one on vellum; a number of valuable books and some fine MSS. Amongst the rest is the first printed edition of the Psalms in 1457, of which we are told the only other perfect copy is in our king's library; that Lord Spencer had only an imperfect copy, and that twelve thousand francs had been already offered for this one volume! So the world goes! This sum would furnish a handsome set of all the best French authors, and amusement for life; but many you find prefer a single black-letter volume, which one must go to school again to learn to read, and which indeed looks like a child's great black-letter spelling book, or the books among the giant friends of Gulliver. A single page as a specimen would, to me, be as good as the whole, and thus five hundred curiosos would be gratified for a few guineas a-head; or a lottery would be still better—fifty pages the highest prize, and a few lines for every one; no blanks! There would be another advantage in this, that it would be employment for some worthy collector for half his life to reassemble all the parts and put the book together again.

The Marquess of Buckingham has been here, and is now going to Tarbes and Barege, and then returns to see our great man.   We hear the latter was at the review at Paris in his blue coat and round hat.   This is quite like him and upon a good   principle; the marshals, the public functionaries, the kings and the emperors, would have outdone anything he could have put on except this.

I am sorry I did not return from Revel through Castelnaudary. Some of the officers did so, and by that means fell in with a division of the French army. The French officers were very civil, but told the same story—"If the Emperor had not deserted us we never would have deserted him; and the men are of the same opinion, but as it was there was nothing else to be done." Colonels B—— and C—— went over to the second review at Montauban, where the Duc d'Angoulême reviewed Count Reille's corps—two divisions. If I had known this had been permitted I should have been very curious to be of the party. I am told the men were well equipped and in high order. The officers in general looked very shabby and unlike gentlemen.

Suchet was smiling and in high good humour, and very fine, as he was here. Soult was only to be distinguished by a most enormous hat, and by a surly look, which is described as unpleasantly penetrating, and more bespeaking talent than amiability. He took little notice of the English officers, but the aides-de-camp and staff-officers, both belonging to Soult and to the other Generals, did so when they learnt who they were, and appeared very earnest in their attentions and civilities. They went there in a carriage, but were splendidly mounted immediately—Colonel —— on Count Erlar's led and caparisoned charger.

Thursday, 12th.—Lord Wellington not having yet returned, and of course nothing positive being known as to our destination, we have only those passing reports which the military men call " shaves."

General Hope is, I fear, likely to suffer long from his wounds. He has astonished the Generals at Bayonne by making three of them presents each of an English horse out of his stud. It is an odd circumstance, but I believe true, that the sort of notice we had of an intended sortie by the enemy at Bayonne, which was given by a deserter just before it took place, only did us mischief. The out pickets were doubled, and as no pickets could stand the rush of four or five thousand men, we only lost so many more prisoners by this. The men were alarmed with the expectation of such an attack. The only fault I hear spoken of in this business was the abandonment of the

church of St. Etienne, which might, and ought to
have been maintained. The fifth division were
but just on duty there, and scarcely knew their
posts. General Hay met the men running back
from it, and was stopping and leading them on
again, saying he would show them how to defend
the church, when he was killed. Some of the
muskets of our men were found there, broken by
the French, and thrown away unfired. An English
officer, with about twenty men, maintained himself in a house near the church the whole time,
though it was much less defensible than the
church.

I am told our position there, close under the
works, was liable to such a sortie every night, and
some well informed, wonder it did not take place
sooner. General Hope's eager courage led him to
be in a situation where, as I am told, no one could,
under ordinary circumstances, remain the shortest
time without almost a certainty of destruction.
Even as it was, it is said a party of Guards ought
to have carried him off, as at first only four Frenchmen were near him when his horse fell, and the
Guards then were close by. The French had
made the outworks of the citadel very strong;

they must have been stormed first, which would have cost us about twelve or fifteen thousand men. It would then have taken sixteen days to establish batteries on the crest of the glacis, the only possible way of breaching the citadel. The garrison, who are now excessively bold, and who have demanded rations for nineteen thousand two hundred men, say they should have even then stood a storming twice—in the citadel, and again in the town at last.

Making all due allowance for this gasconading, it is quite as well to have been saved the necessity of taking Bayonne. It would have taken all our transports about sixteen days to bring up materials for four days upon trenches from Passages by land, and we must then, for the remainder of the time, have trusted to the uncertainty of the water communication. The object of the French sortie was supposed to be the destruction of our three stores of fascines and gabions, &c., which we had been six weeks and more cutting, collecting, and forming, and for which purpose we had stripped the environs for near five miles round the town. In that respect we were quite prepared for the whole siege, and it is remarkable enough that we re-

mained nearly all that time sufficiently near the
French works to form the first parallel, and that
without making works to protect ourselves, because
doing so would only have drawn down a fire which
no works could have enabled us to live under, and
there was nothing to be done but to remain as
quiet as possible until the siege began. Had we
withdrawn at all, the French having seen the importance of the ground, which we got as it were
almost by accident, would have made it necessary
to begin the siege by the storming of the works
they would soon have made there. Thus we
were obliged to keep what we had got, unless
resolved to turn the whole into blockade. The
French engineers admire our bridge very much,
and say it will figure in military history; but
their officers in general in Bayonne have hitherto
been very sulky, and we are by no means friends
as yet. Very little accommodation is afforded us in
any way.

We are infinitely obliged to Bonaparte for
having lost his head, and blundered as he did
latterly, and suffered the Allies to enter Paris, and
put an end to the war. Had he succeeded at
Paris, or had Soult and Suchet united succeeded

against us here, near the shores of the Mediterranean, where our next conflict would have been, you would have found, when a retreat became necessary, and that the French saw that way out of their difficulties, instead of a return to loyalty, that we should have had the other party, and that a strong one, uppermost, and a cry the other way, with parties in our rear, &c. Thinking, as we do, the French army, and a great part of the French nation, quite as much responsible and to blame as Bonaparte, for a considerable portion of the misery caused by France (to effect which they were, as long as it was out of France, his willing agents, and they only deserted him, when he was in distress, because his fortunes had left him, and by no means from principle) thinking this, their excess of loyalty only disgusts us. Of course we are glad to promote it, but must despise the majority of the Bourbon shouters—a few honourable individuals, and a small party, of course, excepted.

Friday, 13th May.—Lord Wellington not yet returned, and our late very warm weather turned to a steady rain. The Paris papers of the 8th, received this morning, make Lord Wellington ambassador in France and Duke.

I was last night at the play to see *La Reine de Galconde,* an opera, with some pretty music. I mention this merely on account of a curious circumstance attending. A French General, according to the story, fights for the deposed Queen, and restores her. The troops of this French General and liberator were a part of the Grenadier company of our Scotch *sans culottes* here in their own costume; and as they marched past, commanded and headed by the French General in the full costume of a general officer of Bonaparte's army, the house immediately applauded the English heroes. The sensations of the French officers present must have been strange, and not very agreeable. These Scotchmen are considered by all the inhabitants (of the town in particular) as having had the principal share in their defeats in sight of the town. The mutes, bearers, and others in the procession, were all English soldiers.

We have had no disturbances or quarrels here, and our officers seem all to have behaved with considerable propriety. In short, the inhabitants dread our departure, and the return of their own people. They say that all order ceases, and all security, the moment our side of the line of demarcation is passed. One furious old gentleman at the *café*, this morning, said publicly, that he thought the only regret was, that the war had not lasted three months longer, to destroy the remainder of the French brigands; and that, as for Soult, he should have been sent in here, that the women might cut pieces out of his flesh with their scissors, and that he might afterwards have been executed publicly for his conduct to this city.

Saturday, Post-day.—Lord Wellington returned in the middle of the night, and, having had a cold, that and his journey make him look rather thin. He has been so taken up with business that I only saw him for a moment. Report says he leaves us again in a day or two. I shall, if I can, ask leave, on our arrival at Bordeaux, to be independent, and find my own way home: yet I believe it would be best to go home with the army.

Head-Quarters, Toulouse, May 21, 1814.—Immediately after my last, Lord Wellington left us for Madrid. Nearly every one has quitted the army; I mean the great men, generals, &c. We are reduced to a few quiet parties, and have no events to observe upon, and see no strangers to write about; everything is tame and stupid, and the weather, growing hot, makes us languid and idle.

Lord Wellington, on his return here, was absolutely overwhelmed with business, and every department was at work in a sort of confusion and hurry, that has never happened before.

On Sunday, the Duke gave a splendid ball and supper at the Prefêt's or Palais Royal, where everything went off much as usual. The ladies dressed well, and danced admirably; and the supper was not a matter of mere form with them. Their early dinners, and their greater exertion in dancing, made them certainly more voracious than our fair ones.

On Monday, the Marquess of Buckingham returned, and was introduced to his new cousin of Wellington. The latter seemed, I understand, not a little surprised at being embraced and saluted on the cheek by his new relative. He had not been in the habit of receiving those embraces *à la mode Française*, and, I take it, prefers very much the kind attention of the fair ones here, with whom he is an universal favourite.

On Monday the Marquess of Buckingham dined

with him, as well as a large party of French and English. I was of the number, and we all went to a concert of very moderate music in the evening at the Capitolium. The Duke at eight the next morning was off for Madrid. He intends to rejoin us at Bordeaux, and then to return through Paris, and to be in London about the 10th of June. This is a great deal too much, and I think almost impossible. These exertions make him look thin and rather worn; but he was very gay, and in excellent spirits whilst here.

The American party was all settled by him finally, and is all on the road to Bordeaux, or now there. It will be of about nine or ten thousand men, I should think, and strong in artillery. Our faithful six eighteen-pounders, which have marched all the way from Lisbon since this day twelvemonth on roads which never have, I think, or will see such animals again, were embarked yesterday on the Garonne, for Bordeaux, to be of the party; and their little grandchildren, the mountain guns, go also. At first the expedition was by no means popular, but is now tolerably so; and the staff appointments have been of course much in request. Lord Fitzroy Somerset, who is the great manager of all this, and prime-minister, has been very busy, and we have all the intrigues of a little court in miniature. Those who have been long here on the staff, and with high brevet rank, will feel much a return to their regimental duty and rank, and still more if their fate be half-pay! I hear of nothing except all this, and the schemes to get provided for. The regimental officers are those who like this new job at least.

The last time I saw the Duke of Wellington I said, I concluded he would wish me to go down to Bordeaux with the army. He answered, "Oh, yes, you had better." We are already almost without Generals. I am told we shall remain here some days yet. The orders, however, are all given for our movement as soon after we receive official news of the garrison of Figueras having marched for France, as possible. In the mean time all wounded, &c., are moving now. The cavalry also are to set out on their way overland to England as soon as the French Government have finally agreed to that arrangement. I should not at all dislike to march with this party. The Portuguese troops remain with the British until the Commissaries can part with the mule transport entirely. They then separate, taking all the mules, muleteers, &c., with them attached to different regiments for rations, &c., and set out through Spain for Portugal, a good three month's trip, growing warmer and warmer all the way, to the great enjoyment, I conclude, of the natives. At Almeyda the muleteers are promised to be paid all their arrears.

The British from hence are to encamp near Bordeaux, ready to be off as transports arrive. The Spaniards move out of France the first of all, at the signal of Figueras, to the joy of all parties. The Guards and troops at Bayonne are likely to be the last, as they are to remain until all stores, wounded, &c., are clear out of the Adour and St. Jean de Luz, &c. The people here will be very sorry to lose us, partly from the loss of the money spent here, and partly from their dread of those who will succeed us—their own countrymen.

I understand General Clausel was the only one of the French here who admitted the truth that they were fairly beaten into taking their King. The others feel it, but will not own it, and are very sulky in consequence; and in general not civil to our officers. Some of the French gensd'armes are expected on Monday in this town to do duty, I believe, to levy taxes, &c. I only hope this will not lead to quarrels with our men.

The continuance of the *Droits réunies* is very unpopular, and I think the effervescence of loyalty is rather going off already. We all expect disturbances also in Spain. I only hope the Duke will resign his command, and have nothing to do with either party. It is said the armies even are divided, and ours here (Frere's) is for the Cortes. What with Spain, Ireland, Norway, America, and perhaps the interior of France, the world will after all, it is feared, not be in that state of profound peace which was generally expected.

Yesterday and to-day I have received letters from you of the 3rd and 10th of May, and papers to the latter date, which contain precisely the same, as to news, as those from London through Paris. There seems to be nothing very important either way.

I have just got the papers relating to a most extraordinary story of a murder at Lisbon. It is a most complete novel, and would be incredibly romantic as such. A Commissary named R——— had an English girl (a lady) who lived with him. Another Commissary named S———, his friend, had

long been living in the same house with him.
After a time Mr. R—— conceived that Mr. S——
was undermining the affections of the lady. He
taxes her with it, she confesses, and says she had
promised to live with S——, but swears nothing
improper had ever passed. Mr. R—— persuades
her to give up this scheme, stating how dishonour-
ably S—— had betrayed him, his friend. He
then tells his friend his discovery, and upbraids
him. S—— says the lady has been faithless to
R——, and is the betrayer. R——, in despair, is
going to quit the house, the lady, and the whole
connexion; but he previously repeats to her what
Mr. S—— told him. She solemnly denies it, and
then goes out with S——. I should have mentioned that the three had just before this conversation ridden out together without speaking, and
sat together at dinner without speaking or eating.
The explanation between R—— and the lady then
took place, immediately after which S—— and
the lady went out of the house. Three pistol-
shots are heard. R—— goes into the garden,
finds his mistress shot dead. S—— ran by him
into the house apparently wounded, his handker-
chief to his head. He forced his way to a table-

drawer, took out a razor and cut his throat quite across. He still survived both wounds when the account came away, and confesses, in writing, deliberately, that by the lady's desire, by their joint consent and agreement, he was to kill both ; her first, and then himself. This he endeavoured to accomplish, but in vain as to himself. Mr. R –— declines telling who the lady is, except in a court of justice, in order to prevent unnecessary pain to her friends in England.

I have been asked, "What is to be done ?" and whether, if the delinquent is mad, I thought that he must be tried for the murder ? It surely was very unfortunate that the poor man had not been left in the hands of the Portuguese surgeons and doctors, who pronounced him a dead man, and his wounds incurable. The skill of an English surgeon has unluckily enabled this unhappy being to stand the chance of either being hung or confined for life as a madman for the rest of his days.

The 22nd, Post-day.—I send you, being dull myself, a part of a *Gazette de France,* which paper I take in regularly. Some part of the *Franc parleur* is well done. The same feelings exist here in the army. Were I a French officer I should feel in the same way.

We have now rain, and the weather cooler again, yet it has not been ever very unpleasantly hot, though at times above our summer heat, and with rain and without sun at 69°.

You ask me in your last letter about religion and manners here? The former seems again much what it was before the Revolution. The churches are in general well attended, but principally (as the case is all over the world, I believe,) by your sex in particular of all ages, by the very old of both sexes, who go there to make their peace; and the very young who are taken there by their older friends and relations. With regard to manners, the old French memoirs would still I think apply very tolerably to the description of their present state, excepting that the same things are done and said with rather more coarseness perhaps now than in old times.

Our cavalry have not moved yet, as the approval of the French government has not arrived. They are intended to move in two columns, one up the Paris road, nearly through Cahors, &c.; the other more to the left, through Angoulême, Poitiers, and to unite at a town on the Seine.

Head-Quarters, Toulouse, May 27th, 1814.—I now eat good dinners, go to the play in the evening, do my business, and take my ride in the morning, and live much such a life as that of all other towns, excepting that my new friends and acquaintance fall off daily around me, and our party at head-quarters is continually on the decline.

I am not a little amused with the Toulouse paper of yesterday. We, the English, have been for these last six weeks praised to the skies, and treated as, and called the deliverers of Toulouse—city and its inhabitants. Soult's troops are now expected in here in a few days, and the gens-d'armes have actually arrived. The Toulouse *Gazette,* therefore, exhorts the inhabitants to receive with open arms and to feast, and entertain those brave troops, whose courage and noble conduct they witnessed on the hills, above this city, when fighting for the defence of the inhabitants, &c.

They also assure the public, the statement in an early number of the *Gazette,* that Marshal Soult

owed the safety of his retreat to the clemency of
Lord Wellington, under whose guns the French
troops filed off, was all an error and mistake (as it
certainly was), and that the retreat was in fact as
secure as the defence of the heights was noble and
courageous. Had we had but about five thousand
more men up, to cross the canal at once, this might
have been another story. The *Gazette* should have
waited until we were off.

I dined yesterday with a Monsieur Catellan, a
gentleman of very good fortune, and who, I understand, has a good house, pictures, library, &c., at
Paris, and lands in Normandy and elsewhere.
He was formerly, at the commencement of the
Revolution, Attorney-general to the Parliament of
Toulouse, and on that account desired to be introduced to me, and gave us an excellent dinner. In
1781, he was a man who figured much here, and
also in the English papers, on account of his early
resistance to the orders of the Court, and being im-
prisoned in consequence. He was followed by all
the inhabitants to his prison, and released in a
short time by the triumph of his own party. He
seems to be a good constitutionalist.

He mentioned several curious facts of Bonaparte's tyranny, such as his putting persons to death without trial, and without inquiry.

Two persons he knew in particular. They were La Vendée chiefs. When all the hopes of that party were gone, terms were offered to these two men. One came in to sign them, when he was instantly shot. The other, in consequence, remained concealed three years in Normandy. At last he was told privately that, that if he would retire from the country quietly, a passport should be given to him. He agreed, received his pass, and made for the coast; but when he had arrived near the seaside, two gens-d'armes shot him.

This made a noise; the Juge de Paix began a *procès verbal*, and the Prefêt was active in endeavouring to apprehend the soldiers. The Judge and Prefêt were not in the secret. Suddenly a senator came from Paris. The Prefêt was suspended from his office and the Juge de Paix enjoined at his peril not to stir a step in the business. Monsieur Catellan's servant acted as clerk in the *procès verbal* which had commenced, and the murder took place close to his estate in Normandy. He therefore, as he said, knew the facts.

Another story, for the truth of which he vouched, and which, from the circumstances, appeared to be true, shows a little the state of Napoleon's court and their morals. A young cousin of Monsieur de Catellan was the Emperor's page—a very good-looking boy. At the carnival he was dressed as a girl at the play, and one of the grand chamberlains fell in love with him. The page continued the disguise and the joke every night during the carnival, and was courted and fêted with presents by the lover. At last the discovery was made, and the mortified chamberlain stopped the boy's promotion in consequence, under the pretence that the page was ordered not to go to the play.

I wished very much to have had time during my visit to Monsieur Catellan to look over a very curious collection of original letters which he had in portfolios, and of which I looked at one or two only. The most valuable were of the Valois family, and were numerous and confidential, coming to Monsieur Catellan through a great-uncle, and derived from an ambassador of the family in Spain. There were several from Catherine de Medicis, mostly about the marriage of her daughters with the Spanish royal family, and which (as she had good occasion to do) she always finished by desiring might be burnt as soon as read.

The eldest daughter was first sent, being intended for the son, Don Carlos, but Philip the Second took a fancy to her, and though the son was in love, married her. An intrigue was suspected with the son, as the daughter was also in love with Don Carlos; the finale was, as history records and romance writers have improved upon, that Don Carlos and the lady suffered death. After this, and knowing, as she must have done, the cause, or at least the reports of all suspected, Catherine writes, saying she must forget the mother in the Queen, and proposing to make up a match between King Philip and her youngest daughter. The letter is a curious one. The writer desires the person addressed to get at the King's mistress and his confessor, and to secure them both as friends to her plans. The remaining letters were only those of eminent men, some from Rousseau, Voltaire, &c., and appeared to contain nothing particularly interesting.

A few days since I think I half made a convert of a fat silversmith's lady here, of whom I was purchasing some articles. She asked me if we had a religion in England at all like theirs. I said, "Yes ; very like." "But," said she (and that weighed very much with her), "you do not use these great silver cups, &c., in your country?" To this I replied, "Indeed we do, and want them much larger than you do in France, as, with us, we let every one taste that pleases of the wine, and you only let the priests." This rather staggered her, when the sale of the cups and sacramental plate came into her head. She then asked what other difference there was? To which I said, "We found a difficulty in being quite convinced that the wine we received and drank at the Communion was actually blood, and though we took it with all due respect as a memorial of the event which was celebrated, yet, after all, we somehow thought the wine was wine—not blood;" to which she could only say that they were bound to believe the contrary, but in her heart I believe she felt much as we do, though she did not dare say so.

May 28, *Saturday, Post-day.*—Our cavalry have at last got their leave to pass through France, and commence their route on the 1st of June. I should imagine we shall move soon after. I have this moment received a packet from you, with papers and enclosures to the 16th, and having your letter now before me, will go through it in answer. The alarms you mention about the quarrels between the Allies, and the French, and the army, and the National Guards, seem to have been principally of English intervention. We have heard little of this matter here, though I have no doubt that the French officers and soldiers are vexed and mortified, and as the Irish say sometimes, they would easily "pick a quarrel" just now, when they meet with any occasion. There is the same feeling here, only as yet scarcely any officers of the army have arrived.

I witnessed last Sunday a quarrel between a gend'arme and a garde urbaine, about cutting off some acacia blossoms in the public walk. The latter was disarmed at last, after a scuffle and fight, in which, from the noise and confusion, you would have supposed several limbs and lives would have been lost (as would have been the case in half the time in England), but in which, in reality, no one seemed to come out the worse. The gend'arme, however, was very neatly beaten at last, as two of the garde urbaine overtook him again, and whilst one tried to wrest the conquered sword back again,

the other cut the belt of the gend'arme, by which
his own sword fell, and in recovering that he lost
the trophy, with which the two lads made off in
triumph.

An officer of the French regular army who was
here by accident a few days since, saw the caricature of Bonaparte in the window, the face made up
of "*victimes*," with the cobweb, &c., introduced,
which I conclude you have seen. He entered the
shop in a rage, and desired the shopman to take it
from the window, threatening to cut him down if
he refused. It has not appeared in the window
since, and the man when now asked for the print
by an Englishman or Royalist, says "They are all
sold."

The Duke of Wellington's misfortune from the
Cossack charge I have not heard of here. He came
back most highly admiring and praising the Russian
cavalry as in appearance the best in Europe, and
saying there was scarcely a private horse in the
regiment he saw, for which a short time ago we
should not willingly have given a hundred and
fifty or two hundred guineas in Spain. The
draught and artillery horses, also, though very
small, and unlike those of the cavalry, he thought

had great appearance of hardiness and activity. Some of your other stories concerning us here are really, I believe, mere inventions.

By-the-bye, what inventions and scandal we shall have now to fill the newspapers and afford conversation for all our idlers ! As soon as peace is signed, they will have little less but that to live upon; whilst the politician must pore over all the debates of the multiplied popular assemblies in modern Europe, which will all be aping our House of Commons.

Our clergy here were ten days ago praying for rain, and they have not sued in vain, as we have had it for this week in showers only, and in the English fashion, not like our mountain and St. Jean de Luz rain. We have also had tremendous storms of wind, which were not prayed for; and more than that, a bit of an earthquake, felt principally at Pau and in that vicinity, but, as I am told, by some perceived here. I do not wonder at old Mother Earth just at first shaking a little at all that has passed lately; but I hope she will take it quietly, and be as peaceably inclined as her inhabitants now are. The recovery of the balance of Europe will be a fine subject for an essay. This superiority over the ancient associated states of Greece, which when once upset never could right themselves again, is a matter of considerable triumph for the moderns, and promises to check for some time another age of barbarism. I should say that one great cause of this has been the more general diffusion of knowledge amongst the middling classes. Public opinion and more fixed principles of the advantages of independence, have got the better at last of a system of universal tyranny of the most ingenious and complicated nature, and extending to every individual, and every hole and corner within its clutches. I must now seal up for the post.

CHAPTER VIII.

PREPARATIONS FOR DEPARTURE—BORDEAUX—IMPOSITION ON
THE ENGLISH—GREETINGS FROM THE WOMEN—MAUSOLEUM
OF LOUIS XVI.

Wednesday, June 1, 1814,
Toulouse.

My dear M——

Here we are still, but on the point of moving. The orders were actually out, and our route fixed. We start on Saturday, the 4th of June, I suspect on purpose to avoid festivities on that day. On the 10th we hope to be at Bordeaux; 4th, Isle en Jordain; 5th, Auch; 6th, Condom; 7th, halt; 8th, Castel Jelous; 9th, Langon; 10th, Bordeaux. This will be sharp work for loaded mules, and warm for us all, as the weather is now clearing up and promises to be hot again.

I am tired of Toulouse, and not sorry to be off, though the inhabitants continue to be civil and friendly. So indeed they ought, as they have made no little money out of us, and have been continually entertained by balls, &c. Since the Duke has been away we have had three balls given by the Adjutant-general, General Byng, and by the aides-de-camp. At the last I was, by accident, introduced to Madame de Vaudreuil. She was, I find, wife to the son of the old admiral, our *émigré* Marquis in England, and your cousin. I was then introduced to the husband and we had some family conversation. He mentioned his nephew, the aide-de-camp in Ireland. He inquired much after the Hochepieds, &c. To-morrow I am to breakfast with them, and you shall hear more. He is a little man, but high, and in repute here.

We have had no events of any consequence. The only thing at all worth mentioning, which I can recollect, is a trait of the conduct of the French lower officers of Soult's army. Two of our officers of the 43rd rode towards Montauban a few days since, out of their own limits, without a passport. This, though foolish just now, was a venial offence, and committed by many French who came in here within our line of demarcation. On a bridge near the town our two gentlemen were met by about eight or ten not gentlemen but officers of the French garrison there. The latter immediately attacked two British officers rudely, told them they ought to know better their own limits, and added at last that if they intended to come again they advised them to come with their coats off, sleeves turned up, and swords drawn. One man actually went so far as to come behind one of our officers to knock his hat off that he might get out the white cockade; in short, the two Englishmen were obliged to yield and return back.

An apology was, I hear, sent in to our General, from the commanding officer at Montauban, saying he was sorry for what had happened, and hoping we would consider it as the act of some *mauvais sujets* in the lower commissioned ranks of the army, and not the act of, or sanctioned by, the garrison in general. I believe, however, we are still to make some remonstrance on the subject.

Dr. Macgregor has returned here, delighted with his trip to Montpelier, Avignon, Nismes, Valence, &c. He was received most cordially everywhere, and at some places quite enthusiastically; almost at every place, he fell in with fêtes and entertainments in consequence of the late changes, and the whole country was covered with conscripts and deserters going home; he thinks he must have seen from ten to twelve thousand. Everywhere, as here, he found much jealousy between the military, the national guards, and the civilians. There were several quarrels in consequence. At the playhouse, at Montpelier, the applause was so violent at a new popular piece called "The Conscript," that a French General, who was there with his suit, conceived it a marked insult to himself, and rose to leave the house, but was persuaded to remain.

The Society of Medicine at Montpelier, made the Doctor a member, with such fine speeches, that, even though he only half understood them, they raised his blushes.

Friday, June 3rd.—In the midst of my bustle and confusion, preparing for my march to-morrow, I received this day your letter and papers to the 24th of May. I had just been reading in to-day's French paper, London news of the same date, so that, even this late mail, of only nine or ten days from London, brought us nothing new, politically, from England. The details, however, and private news are always interesting, and I shall carry the papers with me to study on my journey. I shall

have more occasion for them as I am going the
road on this (the Toulouse) side of the Garonne, instead of our military route, and shall be nearly, if
not quite, alone, as almost every other person who
goes this way intends to travel post, or ride faster
than would suit me this warm weather. I am told
the road I have chosen is by far the most picturesque, rich, and amusing; and, having a passport ready, I mean to start at five to-morrow; I
am to pass through Grisolles, Castel Sarazin,
Monteil, Moissac, Agen, Port St. Marie (where I
shall try and see our *émigré* friend, the Baron de
Trenqueléon), Tomeins, Reolle; then, if necessary,
cross the river to Langon, but if not, keep the right
bank, opposite Bordeaux. I have sent my baggage
and Henry on in the line of march, and only take a
Portuguese, *ci-devant* servant to the Prince of
Orange, and now mine, on a poney, with a small
valise, and intend to trust to the inns for everything. I shall thus avoid troops, and nearly all
places through which they have passed.

The last detachment of cavalry leaves this to-
morrow, to start to Grisolles and Montauban on
Sunday. The Hussars in advance leave Montauban
to-day. The last infantry move from hence on

Sunday; and the whole infantry from hence will be assembled at Bordeaux (excepting what may be embarked) by the 17th of June. The last Portuguese will pass Bayonne about the 23rd; and then the Guards and troops there will be at liberty to move—not before. The Spaniards are nearly all out of the country already!

Sir W. W. Wynne has been here these last five or six days, to succeed the Marquess of Buckingham; they are specimens of our supposed greatest peers and commoners. The people here stare at them, and look strange. The inhabitants are seriously sorry for our departure, I really believe. We had a sort of farewell party at the Duke's house yesterday, given by Colonel C. Campbell—all the great men here—we dined, then went to the play, then to the ball. Some of our Generals are so pleased that they talk seriously of returning again here after peace is signed, and they have laid by their laurels in England. I have so many things to do, that I must now end this, and leave it to go by the post, as I shall be away from head-quarters, and the regular post, perhaps, next mail. Do not be surprised if you do not hear again very soon. I shall try and write the moment I arrive at Bordeaux, and let you know my plans as soon as I can fix them.

Head-Quarters, Bordeaux, June 13*th,* 1814.— On Saturday (11th), I sent you a few hasty lines, I will now try and fill up the interval from Toulouse here, with an account of my proceedings during that time.

After a tremendous thunderstorm, at six in the morning of the 4th of June, I started along the rich plain in which Toulouse stands, and proceeded through Grisolles, and a number of small places, to Castel Sarazin, and not liking the appearance of the latter, I went on to Moissac, which is just across the Tarn, and at which place the plain ceases, and the road becomes hilly.

It was about forty-five miles to Moissac, all rich and fertile, but the country much too bare of wood, and the uniform level road is tiresome from the sameness. The river ran the whole way, about half a mile from the road, and the opposite bank being high, bounded the view on that side, and formed the prettiest object, though not the most profitable, as the soil seemed less rich. The flat lands must be subject to great losses and damage from floods, as there is no fall for the sudden torrents which descend. The corn in many places had suffered much this year.

I passed at Grisolles the last of the cavalry (the Blues), on their way home. The Life Guards entered Montauban with laurels. The Prefêt immediately told the commanding officer, that he understood his men were come into the town in a triumphant manner, and seemed much vexed, until reminded that it was the 4th of June, when he was civil, and admitted the validity of the reason. At the village of Fignan, where I stopped to give my horses some corn, I was very glad to find the inhabitants regretting the departure of the Portuguese regiment which had been quartered there, they had behaved so well. They told me the people cried when they crossed the water, and the next day so many soldiers came back to take another farewell of their new friends, that the officers were compelled to place a guard to prevent it.

The Tarn, at Moissac, was wide, and the current very strong. The passage by the ferry, a troublesome one, backwards and forwards, through the remains of the ruined buttresses of an old bridge. On landing, I asked for the Commandant, or

French General. There had been unpleasant alter-
cations of late, near that place and neighbourhood.
The officer of whom I inquired, pointed to General
Rey, the late governor of St. Sebastian, who hap-
pened to be near. I announced myself to him.
He was civil; and I went to the inn immediately.

The only sights in the town are a great water-
mill in the river, with about twenty-four pair of
mill-stones, and a number of establishments for
purifying wheat and preparing flour. These last
were on a large scale, but without machinery of
any ingenuity, and one steam-engine would have
saved them nearly all their labour, which was
great. The country round is famous as a corn
country, and Moissac was once a great place of
export for flour and wheat by the canal, &c., to
Toulouse, to Montpelier, and by the Tarn and
Garonne to Bordeaux, and thence to the French
islands and foreign settlements, &c. The inhabitants wished much to begin dealing with the
English; but I told them our parliament was
about to prevent that taking place.

There is a curious old church at Moissac with
many carved figures, grotesque enough at the entrance. The style is nearly the old English, but

in some places the early Gothic.   The accommodation at the inns is very good ; but the joke of Milord
Anglais has commenced, and is increasing fast.   We
were all *mon Commandant* and *mon Général;*
and we paid accordingly.

The next day, on leaving Moissac, I ascended a
long hill, and continued on rich high ground above
the river, in a country of cultivated, undulating
scenery, with more wood, somewhat resembling
Devonshire or Somersetshire, with the exception
of the want of hedges.   This continued about seven
miles, when I came down again, having a fine
view of the river, and continued my way along the
banks over a rich flat through several villages and
small towns to Agen, about thirty-four miles from
Moissac.   The valley was here much narrower and
varied than that at Toulouse, bounded on both
sides by gentle hills, cultivated and rich, as well as
apparently populous, along the whole way.   The
French troops were in cantonments in every village,
and looked very sulky in general.   A few touched
their caps to me, as I was in my scarlet uniform ;
but most looked sulky and took no notice.   I was,
however, never insulted.   The cries of the children
all the way, and often of the country-women, and

sometimes of the men, of *vivent les Anglais!* certainly did not contribute to put their soldiers and officers in better humour. If so disposed, I could easily have as the Irish say, " picked a quarrel."

At Agen, all was gaiety and bustle. It was the Sunday before their great fair. All was preparing for that, as well as for the service which was to take place in the great church the next day for Louis XVI., the Queen, &c. I immediately went to the Commandant of the town. He was civil, but the numerous officers looked very much disposed to be impertinent, if occasion should offer. The eager curiosity of the townspeople to see the English, and to be civil, was very pleasing; every one anxious to show some attention. I here fell in with Dr M—— and Mr. and Mrs. J——, and after dining together, we went to the play.

It was a little narrow theatre, but almost new, and very clean and neat. The performances were not despicable. There was a good-looking singer, with no bad voice, from Bordeaux. In her character, much happened to be said of her innocence and inexperience. From the constant joking this gave rise to in the audience, and from some very prominent feature in her person, I conclude she had lately been under the necessity of retiring from Bordeaux, from some little *faux pas*. And this, as I was told afterwards, was the case.

Agen is an old and rather shabby town of about ten or eleven thousand inhabitants; the walks around it, and country, are pretty. The next morning I staid until after the ceremony had commenced in the church, and peeped in, to see what was going on, and if the military attended. Many of the latter did so, with crapes round their arms. I was admitted instanter, without a ticket, and the old priests, several of whom had been *émigrés,* and spoke a little English, were very civil. About twenty milliners had made really a very elegant linen and crape mausoleum for the occasion, nearly twenty feet high. Four fluted pillars, one at each corner, were made of fine white linen, the festoons round the base were of black and white crape, urns on the pillars, and other ornaments of the same. About a hundred and fifty wax candles were up the steps on every side of the tomb, and above it were lilies springing fresh from the centre, and the crown, in elegant crape, suspended above the whole.

About ten o'clock I started again to find out the

Baron de Trenqueléon at Port St. Marie, which was about twelve miles from Agen. On inquiry at the inn, I found there a friend of his son's, who had left him only a few hours before. I, therefore, determined to cross the river again, go and see him, and to stay there the night. Trenqueléon Chateau is about five miles from Port St. Marie, on the road from thence to Nerac, on the side of the hills which enclose the valley in which the Garonne descends. It is old-fashioned in the Tuileries style, and in appearance large. In reality it does not contain much room, but is a comfortable place.

Excepting two higher wings, it is, in fact, only a ground-floor house. The rooms are lofty, spacious, and decently-furnished for a French house in the country. There is a great square garden in front, like a wilderness full of weeds, with a square plantation and straight walks. The roads run about two hundred yards from it on one side, and a small river navigable for boats on the other, and running into the Garonne about four miles below. This would be convenient to export the produce, if there were a market, which of late had not been the case.

I found the old Baron feeble, without the use of
his limbs, in a great chair penned in like a child.
He was surrounded by a large party—his wife, his
son, and his son's wife, daughter to the maire of
Agen; an old lady, I took for the Baron's sister;
and five young ones, who called him "Papa."
One of these was in weeds, and one about twenty-
five or thirty; the rest young.   One was a fresh,
ruddy, English-looking girl.   All were most attentive and civil.   The old Baron made me repeatedly
kiss him, and cried several times as he conversed
with me.   He remembered all our old friends in
England during his emigration.   He was very
anxious to know all I could tell him of my
brothers: He asked much after your sister and
brother, and the T—— family.   His table was
bad, but there was quantity, and a hearty welcome.
I was put into his uncle's room, our old friend the
Bishop of Montpelier's.   His family seemed attentive to him, and, excepting at meal times, seemed
to live around him, some at work, some reading
the papers to him, and some sitting ready to talk,
and with no other occupation.   The poor girls
must lead a very dull life in the Chateau de Trenqueléon, as, from the state of the Baron's health

they do not go out to balls or amusements even at Agen.

On the following morning, I left Trenqueléon about twelve o'clock, and crossed the river again at a ferry near Aiguillon, which is a pretty town, small, but well situated. I got on to Tomeins that night. The country continues to be the same rich valley the whole way and very populous. Tomeins is a small ill-built town of perhaps about five thousand inhabitants. There is nothing to see there, excepting a fine sort of Richmond-terrace view from the public walk overhanging the river. The women struck us as very pretty, and they were peculiarly eager about *" les Anglais,"* one or two calling out in English, as we passed near the windows where they were, " How you do ? how you do ?" &c., and then running away to hide themselves. And this came from well-dressed girls in good houses.

On the 8th I proceeded through Marmande de la Reolle, to breakfast ; and then crossing the river again near Langon, I intended to stop at the pretty village of Barsac, about five miles on this side Langon, and where the good wine of that name comes from. Finding all this part full of our sixth division, just arrived, I was obliged to push on to Ceron, a mere post stage and a poor inn.

On the 9th I proceeded to this place (Bordeaux,) and arrived by one o'clock, when my order to proceed to Tarragona (for the trial of Sir J. Murray) was put into my hands. I found every one in the same hurry and confusion as when the Duke paid his last visit at Toulouse.

The country continued nearly the same until we got some way beyond Barsac; we then began to skirt the Landes, and had only sand and firs, a sort of Bagshot Heath, but still broken by frequent villages and chateaux, which round Bordeaux are very numerous.

During my journey I always stopped at some small inn for a feed of corn in the course of the way, and also during rain, which was frequent and heavy. I gave the chance passengers their wine to make them talk. A drunken Frenchman seemed much like an English one, and was sometimes very entertaining; but the feeling of the soldiers was the most curious. At one place I found two discharged soldiers going home with their leave; they said they had been betrayed by their

Generals, &c., and the game was up, so they had applied for their discharges, as they would not fight for the King.   They had served seven or eight years, and would now be quiet, though their wounds would not have prevented their fighting for the Emperor.   One had lost a finger only, the other had received a knock in the leg, which rather made him halt a little; they had both above sixteen months' pay due to them, but said they concluded of course the King would never pay the Emperor's debts, and they were satisfied to be discharged without pensions.   They said that nine-tenths of the soldiers of the army would have remained firm to the Emperor if their Generals had been faithful, and had agreed in opinion with them; " *mais n'importe, c'est fini.*"

The Trenqueléon party told me, they were for some time in great uneasiness, as we had no troops near them on their left bank of the river, and on the right bank only came down to the river Lot. Thus Agen was the centre of the formation of partisan corps who were to cross the river near them, and scour the country to annoy us.

In three or four instances they succeeded in this; and the Commissioner was issuing most violent orders to compel all persons to form their corps immediately (these if caught by us would be hung) and to teach the women also, to entice into their houses our soldiers by wine, &c., to make them prisoners and kill them, and even to instruct their children to cut the back sinews of the horses in the stables at night, saying they must do as the Spaniards did by them in Spain.

The Baron's family said they had different feelings, but would have been compelled to do much of this, had things gone on. They also talked with much horror of the state of terror they had been kept in by Bonaparte's agents. One deputy Prefêt, some time since, alarmed them by quietly telling some of their neighbours (who told them again) that they were in a terrible scrape, and had been detected corresponding with the English. They went instantly to the Prefêt to know what this meant, and found it was one of my father's letters about the Bishop of Montpelier's affairs, (as his executor in England), which had been stopped by the police. The Prefêt afterwards told him to be easy " *ce n'était rien.*" The Baron seems to have been a popular character in the neighbourhood.

12*th, later.*—A mail goes to-day, and I have a

pile of papers a foot high to arrange by to-morrow. The Duke goes away and leaves the army the day after, Wednesday the 14th, consequently all is a bustle of business, balls, dinners, operas, plays, all proceeding at once. My next will give you an account of this handsome town. I am in quarters at Monsieur Emerigon's a barrister now at Paris, but daily expected to return. The Duke has written strongly home to put off this intended Court-martial at Tarragona; all here detest it, and grumble. The worst is, that we are to remain here in suspense until an answer arrives.

I am writing without my coat, and so are all the Duke's Secretaries, &c., from the heat. The thermometer shut up in my writing-desk is at 76°. The sun most ardent when out.

CHAPTER IX.

THE OPERA-HOUSE—THE CATHEDRAL—THE SYNAGOGUE—A
JEWISH WEDDING—STRANGE SHOW-HOUSE—WELLINGTON
AND KING FERDINAND.

Head-Quarters, Bordeaux,
June 16, 1814.

My dear M——

As I have no news to communicate, you
must be satisfied with the best account of Bordeaux
which the excessive heat permits me to give you.
The Duke is gone for good, and we are left here in
a state of dull, and I may say feverish uncertainty.
Time slips away fast, and my fate will soon be
decided.

Before breakfast I take an hour's ride to look
about the town and suburbs, and see what I could
not do otherwise. I have commenced a new plan,
early dinner solo, and another ride in the evening,
or the opera; this is my life. The restaurateurs
are so hot! I prefer my own society and a mutton

chop with abundance of vegetables and fruit, and my bottle of claret or Sauterne to the incessant dinners going on in public. My wine I get from the housekeeper of my landlord, Monsieur Emerigon the counsellor, as she in his absence sells his produce for him—his wine, namely Sauterne Emerigon, which is really very good, his pigeons, his ortolans, his poultry, his cherries, his vegetables, &c. As he is not yet returned from Paris, I have also taken possession of his *salle à manger*, and drawing-room, in addition to my bed-room. I only now want to get into his library. He is a royalist, and one of the commissioners sent from Bordeaux to Paris.

Bordeaux is a very handsome town, and very superior to Toulouse—as a city indeed there is no comparison; but still I think there was more *ton* and fashion at Toulouse. This place was stopped by the Revolution, when in a state of splendid commercial prosperity; it was then rapidly increasing in magnificence. Toulouse on the contrary, I take it, was even then on the decline. Another advantage Bordeaux has in addition to its having been laid out like Bath with modern improvement as to the width of the streets, namely the convenience of stone quarries close at hand, instead of bricks to form the buildings, and this with water carriage. It has besides a stone somewhat similar to Portland stone, a complete Bath stone cut by the saw and adze like that at Bath; and of course these advantages have not been neglected by Frenchmen.

The river is a noble one, not very much wider than the Thames at London Bridge, but it appears deeper, and of more importance; the tide occasionally reaches up as high as near Langon. I should suppose the quays extend nearly two miles, and, in general, are well-built and handsome, and the river just now is full of shipping. The quays are inferior to those at Lyons, and the few half-rotten ships on the stocks in the spacious yard, show strongly the urgent necessity of what the people did on the late occasion.

The Grand Theatre is a very handsome building, with a colonnade of twelve pillars in front. The whole height of the building, and with its connections of taverns, Exeter Change, &c., runs back to the river. In its front is a square, with two handsome streets branching off right and left, One has the double row of trees, in the foreign fashion, in the centre, with paved carriage-roads outside, and is spacious, ornamental, and useful. At the end of this is the other Théâtre de la Gaieté, and that leads into a sort of wide avenue street planted all the way, and nearly a mile long. On one side again of this is the *ci-devant* Champ de Mars, or Jardin Publique, a spacious public planted walk. The town contains several other planted wide streets, and a handsome Palais-Royal, *ci-devant* Du Prefêt. There is not any one very handsome square, and upon the whole I prefer Brussels—a town, I should think, nearly of the same size.

The Opera House is in the inside handsome, but dirty, and not well contrived as to holding numbers. It consists of twelve large Corinthian pillars, which occupy much of the room, and all the upper boxes are like baskets projecting between them, and only two deep. The shape of the house a flat horse-shoe, and well proportioned. The singing tolerably good; the dancing by no means despicable. Excepting, perhaps, one or two of our best, it is better than at our London theatres. The dresses are rich and expensive. The reception of our Duke was very gracious; and it was not a little curious to hear " God save the King" sung constantly with

"*Vive Henri IV.!*" *A l'Anglais, à l'Anglais,* was also a popular cry, and produced a hornpipe tune, always attended with great acclamation, but what the connection was I cannot say. Some impudent sailors always cried out for "Rule Britannia," but French *politesse* could not go so far. Two Americans would not pull off their hats one night to "God save the King," and were shouldered out in consequence.

The upper boxes are entirely filled with very smartly-dressed ladies of a certain class, whose wardrobes have improved in the last two months, I have no doubt, as much as that of the similar class of ladies at Toulouse,—and the last was very visible. The Théâtre de la Gaieté is a sort of Sadler's Wells, neither more elegant, nor more chaste. The rope-dancing is decidedly good. There is also a Musée here, as well as at Toulouse, but much inferior. There are not half a dozen original pictures of any tolerable master. The antique inscriptions are very uninteresting, to me at least, and there were no antiques affording pleasure to an artist or amateur. The collection of birds, serpents, butterflies, minerals, &c., tolerable, but only of the second order. I think the library also appeared smaller and inferior to that at Toulouse, but there were many more r aders, which surprised me.

There is also a deaf and dumb establishment here similar to that at Paris, and a very intelligent master apparently, and very civil. I staid there two hours, to have a regular lesson of the principles of the education illustrated by the female pupils, who were the most forward. There were about seventy scholars, mainly supported by the government. The pupils were not quite so skilful as those at Paris, but it is always an interesting exhibition. To find out what we were, the teacher ingeniously made a pupil ask us what nation we were of, and of what profession, and as all the deaf and dumb pupils rejoiced in the answer, and seemed much pleased, I determined to keep up our good character, and gave the damsels a Napoleon, for which I got much dumb-show thanks in return.

The cathedral, or principal church, of St. André, is a good Gothic building of about the second class, built by "*vos Messieurs les Anglais,*" as we are instantly told. It is in one respect unfinished, as both the north and south fronts are intended to

have each two light Gothic spires on the towers,
whereas, only one pair is built,—the other has but
just commenced. The pair that exist were some
little time since out of repair, and a part had fallen
down. Bonaparte saw this, and graciously said
they must be put in order directly. The Bourde-
lois were grateful, thinking he intended having it
done, but he only ordered it, and a tax on the
commune at the same time, to pay for it. In the
same way, as he came from Lyons to Bordeaux, he
found the road bad, and much out of repair : this
he also ordered to be repaired immediately, but an
impôt all along the communes on the road, beyond
the expense of the repairs, followed likewise as
immediately. The Prefêt's palace he also ordered
to be put in complete order, and it was just
finished in time to receive the Duc d'Angoulême,
which was not quite according to the wishes and
intentions of the said Bonaparte.

The Exchange at Bordeaux is a well-contrived
handsome building, and the square in the centre,
roofed in, with sky-lights, to form a convenient
place for the different walks. The cloisters round
are full of shops, jewellery, maps, &c.

June 28th.—I have just returned from the synagogue, where I have been these two hours. There are nearly two thousand Jews at Bordeaux. "It is no wonder the Christians are well fleeced," as my French companion observed. "when there are two thousand persons in the town who impose it upon themselves as a duty, and cheat for religion's sake." The chapel is a new building, the style of architecture not good, being a sort of imitation of Saxon, or rather of no particular order, but the shape of the temple is excellent, the proportions good, and the whole imposing. A colonnade, formed by pillars runs all round, with a gallery above for the women, who are separated from the men. The altar at the end, with the ark of the covenant and the books of Moses, &c. The branch in the centre; round this the reading-desks, with the rows of lights for the priests, &c. The upper gallery is arched over like Covent Garden, with a circular roof.

The Jews were very civil. The singing was tolerably good; the singing boys, about twenty in number, in white surplices and sky-blue silk sashes and scarfs, and bonnets, had a good effect, mixed with the old priests in their hoods. The producing the books of Moses and returning them to the ark were the most imposing ceremonies in point of solemnity, and music; but what to me was the most striking, was when, at a certain period in the service called the Benediction, every parent found immediately his son or grandson, or the children their parents. In short, after a few moments' bustle, you saw every one, whatever his age, imposing his hooded head and hands on his own offspring, and every generation thus at the same instant receiving the benediction from his own parent respectively. This was really an imposing scene.

The most truly Jewish part followed, for by solemn proclamation every sacred office, namely, the opening of the ark, the drawing the curtains, carrying the books, putting on the ornaments, reading out of them when produced, the right of assisting in every part of the ceremonies, was regularly put up to auction, and sold to the highest bidder. The biddings were from one franc to three and five, and even at times up to forty and fifty. As I was informed, these profits were given to the poor. There was a little spoilt Jew child, about six years old, for whom its papa had, I conclude, bought the privilege of placing the silver ornaments on the tops of the wooden rollers of the vellum Pentateuch, and the little creature seemed much pleased and excessively proud of his office. On Wednesday next there is a wedding, and if not engaged I intend to be present.

The coffee-houses here, before we came, were very good, and are not very dear. They are now so hot and crowded, and in such confusion, that I prefer my dinner solo. Being in a great measure fixed by *la carte* as to prices, I believe we are less imposed upon at the restaurateurs than anywhere else.

I rode out one day about four miles on the old Bayonne road, to see a house and garden much talked of here, belonging to a Mons. R——, the Portuguese Consul, a queer old man, who goes about here in a scarlet uniform, like our former English Generals, and with a white-feathered General's hat. The grounds and gardens are large, and in the first style of a Paddington tea-garden, with a mixture of Hawkstone nonsense and Walsh Porter's sham villages, &c. The house is nothing remarkable, consisting of a number of rooms by no means good; not a single good picture, only some bad indecent ones, and very free prints. The

most ludicrous part was a regular inscription of
" Library" over a door which led to a little closet
with one small set of book-shelves, containing
much such a library as that at *   * *, namely, a
dozen or two of great almanacs and a few odd
volumes of all sorts of books, the whole in number
about a hundred.

On the landing-place on the stairs is a negro,
carved in wood, holding a bottle and glass. The
flower garden, in the old style, is tolerable. There
are no good statues, but plenty of cut trees in all
shapes, temples, &c., the whole an endeavour to
make poor nature as little likely to know herself
as possible. There were trees with the stems in
frames and the tops pointed. In the cut pro-
menades in the woods were tombs and wooden
painted figures, of all sorts and descriptions. There
were dogs in their houses, the prodigal son feeding
swine, a mad lady half naked in a cage, &c. In
another part of the garden was a labyrinth, and a
windmill with a wooden man looking out of one
window and a woman out of the other, and below
these a wooden cow and some sheep, goats, deer, of
the same material, grazing.

Strangers are admitted to survey this place on

any day. The doors were opened to about a dozen of us, and we were turned loose, without any show-man, into the house and grounds, and ranged about where we pleased. On Sunday every one is admitted, and I am told there is much company. The walks are cool, and I am not surprised at their being frequented. The whole is one way out of many of obtaining notoriety. An ingenious way of preserving the flowers is by an inscription insinuating that every flower is a transformed female. This would not, I fear, succeed in England. The poor ladies would have many a pinch and squeeze, and lose many a limb, if Kensington Gardens were full of such flowers and had no other protector.

Sunday, 19*th*.—Our embarkation is now going on with more spirit. The fourth division are, I believe, all on board, if not sailed, and everything is, by degrees, moving down towards the camp, at Blanquefort, and the place of embarkation, Rouillac, about thirty-five miles below this. From my state of uncertainty I shall be one of the last, if I go at all, that is if our Tarragona Court-martial is put an end to. All accounts I have heard agree with P—'s. I have thought all along that, with the help and assistance of Bonaparte himself, who was our best ally, the whole of what has happened nearly has arisen, as it were, from the peculiar state of the nations of Europe, and from a natural course of events directed by Providence, and with which the Allies had nothing to do, but not to prevent it by their blunders or quarrels.

We have various letters from Toulouse, to officers of the army, full of regret for the loss of their English friends, and by no means satisfied with the exchange for their own countrymen. The army is vexed at this, and matters are worse, as they do nothing but grumble and quarrel in consequence. I hear the reception of the French troops when they entered was very flat and provoking. D'Armagnac, who was supposed to have saved the town, by advising Soult to be off, was sent in first, with two thousand five hundred men, and he and his officers bowed, and were very anxious to court a cordial greeting; but the dull silence was scarcely broken, and the French officers could not contain their vexation and abuse in consequence. I believe there was more sincerity in the professions of the Toulousians towards us, as far as the majority was concerned, than is usual with Frenchmen, or than we could reasonably have expected from them.

On the other hand, the accounts from the cavalry of their treatment in their march through France is very different from ours at Toulouse. In this they all agree. The officers, trusting to French hospitality, have left their own beds behind, and having had to bivouack almost as much as in Spain, they have had a bad time of it. Several letters have come from Mr. H——, who went with the column through Angoulême and Poictiers. He has written from both these places. He says, " The inhabitants profess openly that, as we chose to march through France, they will try and make us repent of it. They scarcely give any quarters, send the men leagues about out of the road, and only let the Commissary buy his provisions on the road. At Angoulême, a town which might quarter ten thousand men, without inconvenience, for a short time, they would suffer only a few officers and the General in the town, and most of those were quartered at inns. The General and one servant got a billet at a private house, but he was to pay if he took more in with him. The incivility is general ; the doors

all shut against us. The playhouse at Angoulême
was empty the night it was known our officers
would be there. Nothing to be had without paying." This is the same spirit of vexation as that
in the army—a sensation of conviction that they
have been beaten, and that this march is a sort of
proof, and token of it.

Head-Quarters, Bordeaux, June 26th, 1814.—
My life has been every day the same—a ride early,
at work at home all the middle of the day, a dinner
generally solo, and another walk or ride in the
evening, or, as our weather has become cooler
again, sometimes the play.

I have spoken to Colonel M—— about your
friends who think of a removal to the south of
France, he having many connexions at Toulouse.
He is decidedly of opinion that that should be the
place of abode, for a family of ladies especially; I
am rather disposed to be of the same opinion. Pau,
however, which I have not seen, is much recom-
mended. Supposing they fix on Toulouse, Colonel
M—— says of course that the house which they
will require for comfort must be a large one, giving
them four rooms with *lits de maître,* and four beds
for *filles de chambres,* and about four other ser-

vants, and three good sitting-rooms, &c.; he thinks
such a house may be had for about eighteen hundred francs a year, that is about 75l. a year. I
can assure them, that in point of economy, all must
depend upon their arrangements being made by
some French friends, and not by an English one.
In house-rent, in wine, in everything, an inhabitant
will get articles at one-third of the price demanded
of the English. The French have no ideas of
honesty or moderation towards the English, and not
much towards any one in matters of trade. The
extortion, and even the downright frauds committed, especially on travellers, are quite disgraceful, and every tradesman assists his neighbour
in getting a job, and fleecing the *milords*. I believe they are like the Jews, and have, from continued practice, arrived at the same conclusion as
the others from religion, namely, that they are per-
forming a duty when they cheat an Englishman.

There are two Protestant chapels here, and one
excellent preacher, in the style of a London chapel
preacher, only extempore; I heard one very elo-
quent French sermon delivered by him, with great
propriety. The service, the singing, and other parts
of the duty are but moderately performed.

The courts of justice are much the same as at Toulouse, and about nine or ten judges generally attend. I was unfortunately obliged to leave Toulouse before their criminal sessions with a jury commenced, and when I arrived here they were over. This takes place only once in three months, unless something extraordinary or a great press of business occurs. I attended a case of misdemeanor, a bad assault, in the criminal court, but that was an appeal only, and being of the class of *petits délits*, there never is a jury, a president and five judges only. The same number presides when there is a jury, in more penal trials; and in certain cases when the jury are divided, as, for instance, seven against five; the judges then are called in to vote as jurymen, and the proportion of votes required by law calculated on the whole numbers. There was much unnecessary delay and argument in the case I heard. It was like one of our worst managed cases of motions for a new trial on account of deficiency of evidence, which are always of the most tiresome class.

Post-day, June 27th.—I have been to the Jew's wedding. The ceremony consists principally of singing and drinking, and blessings in Hebrew. There must be something Jewish, however, as usual, and that is concerning the ring, which, as soon as it is produced, is shown round to all the rabbies near, and some elders, &c., and to the sponsors, to be sure it is really gold, or otherwise the marriage is void, and the true old clothesman-like way in which they all spied at the ring was very amusing. Nearly the last ceremony is the bridegroom's smashing a wine-glass in a plate on the floor, with an idea that he and his spouse are then as difficult to separate as it would be to reunite the glass. The gentleman showed gallantry by exerting all his force, and looking most fierce, as he broke the glass.

I understand the Duke of Wellington came back from Madrid with a much better impression of King Ferdinand than when he went, thinking that he showed talent, firmness, and character. The manner in which he received the Duke may have somewhat disposed him to this favourable judgment. I understand the King immediately treated the Duke as a Grandee of Spain by shaking hands with him and putting his hat on, and that the King declared almost the only two acts of the Cortes, which he approved of *in toto,* were those which made the Duke commander of all the

Spanish armies, and gave him the estate in the south.

We have had news from our cavalry from the vicinity of Paris, from Chartres; all the officers have deserted their regiments to see Paris—that present wonder of wonders! They have occasionally lately been better treated, that is, whenever they met with a Royalist patron at their quarters. H—— says there seems to be two parties everywhere, and it is a sort of lottery which they fall into the hands of; that, when he wrote last from Chartres he had been "stuffed to death," made to eat three or four meals a-day, and to attend a party given on purpose for him every evening: this, I conclude, was all a *douce* violence.

Still no news as to our Tarragona plan. My patron, Monsieur Emerigon, says that at Paris the Emperor of Russia, individually, was the most popular, excepting perhaps the English and our Duke; that the Russian troops were not in such favour; the King of Prussia so-so, Blucher and his troops better, but the Emperor of Austria the worst of all; and every one must have observed the marked difference of his reception from that of the other sovereigns.

I am to-day turned out of my room, which is the dining-room, as my patron gives a dinner. I am asked to dine with him. I must not therefore complain, but must finish to clear away for the entertainment in good time.

We have been paid up a good deal of money at this place, where the quantity of gold and silver we have circulated is quite incredible. Every one talks of it, and the piles and piles of empty money-boxes of all sorts, and from all quarters, fully prove it. At present we have immense quantities of French money, Napoleons and Louis gold and silver, from Paris, whilst, on the other hand, I am told the French are here buying up our guineas and Portuguese gold, to turn them into Louis, as they have begun a new coinage both here and at Paris.

CHAPTER X.

COUNTRY FETES—BRAWLS WITH THE FRENCH—THE DUC D'AN-
GOULEME—MADEMOISELLE GEORGES—THE ACTRESS AND THE
EMPEROR—FRENCH ACTING AND FRENCH AUDIENCES—PRE-
SENTATION OF A SWORD TO LORD DALHOUSIE—GEORGES'
BENEFIT—DEPARTURE.

> Head-Quarters, Bordeaux, July 4, 1814,
> Post-day.

My dear M——

WE have still had no instruction, and are
waiting the determination in England; in the
mean time I am now gradually stewing away, as
the heat has again commenced, and is in full operation. My life is quite retired and monotonous,
and affords no incidents. The only variety that
has arisen is, that yesterday I dined at three
o'clock with my patron's sister, a West Indian
elderly single lady, and a female party. I was the
only beau, as the brother was engaged, and in the
evening I rode over about three miles to Briges, a
village, where they were keeping an annual fête.

The crowd of country people dancing and singing was very considerable, and the road there was covered with the lower class going, and returning. The difference between this and our country fêtes seem to be, that there was nothing to buy or sell, and but little eating and drinking going on, the principal occupation being dancing and talking, laughing and parading about. It seems impossible to make such a people as the French very unhappy in any way (however bad their government) except by the conscription.

Those who are satisfied with salads, sour wine, dancing, and other amusements entirely depending upon themselves and the meeting of the two sexes, can only be disappointed and deprived of their happiness by the removal of one sex altogether. Leave them alone, and they have nearly all they wish. John Bull on the contrary wants many things more to put him into the same state of joy and satisfaction.

Several of Marshal Soult's officers have got into Bordeaux of late; disputes and quarrels have been the consequence, but as yet of no great moment. Every opportunity of seeking a row was eagerly laid hold of by the French—a jostle on the stairs at the play was sufficient. Lord Dalhousie (in command here now) has been obliged to forbid any officer going to the Théâtre de la Gaieté where this was most likely to arise, and to order off every officer not on duty here to camp. We have now only the Guards here, and staff officers. The inhabitants are all with us, particularly a set of very fine-looking young men, but a little hot-headed, who compose the Duc d'Angoulême's guard of honour. They have been also insulted, and a few days since paraded with bludgeons to see if this would be repeated either as against themselves, or the English, and they determined to resist either on the spot. No great harm has happened as yet. As far as I can learn, there have been about three fights, but none fatal.

A young Tyrolean in the pay office department was insulted; he watched and followed the offender home; then went for his sword (which we never wear and the French always), returned, and insisted upon instant satisfaction; the Frenchman's zeal began to cool, but it was too late; the Tyrolean made him go out into a back-yard and fight directly, cut him across the face, and was just about running his sword into his body, when a friend interfered, and stopped him, saying "he had done enough."

Another Frenchman has been horse-whipped by an English officer, who when insulted returned with his sword and whip, and offered the Frenchman his choice, and as the latter persisted in asking for time, he chose for him, and gave him the whip. All this makes Lord Dalhousie anxious to get the troops off, and as I hear Lord Keith has promised plenty of transports in answer to his pressing letters on the subject we are expected to be nearly all away in ten days' time, and some immediately. There are nearly eighteen thousand men still in France, including the fifth division at Bayonne, where by-the-bye the disposition on the part of the French to be uncivil, sulky, and quarrelsome has been much greater. On the contrary the Generals and superior officers are very civil, Marshal Suchet particularly so, to the few of our officers who remained at Toulouse, and General Villette, who is here, is the same.

Later.—A ship is just arrived in sixty-four hours from Plymouth, telling us fifteen sail of the line, and as many frigates are close at hand, but no news of our destination.

Head-Quarters, Bordeaux, July 10*th*, 1814.
—I have now received two letters and packets
of papers from you by the last mail, including
those up to the 28th June. This same mail
brought orders for all the members of the Court-
martial appointed for Tarragona to proceed direct
for England, and there report themselves to the
Adjutant-general. Upon this I asked Lord Dalhousie
(our present chief) what I was to do? and was by
him desired to remain here to the last and move
with the head-quarters, who remain here till the
troops move. This must, I think, take place in
about a week or ten days, unless you cease to send
shipping from England. We shall in three days'
time have only a brigade of Guards remaining for
the city duty. The rest who will not be already
embarked will be at Poulliac in readiness.

We have now got our small share of royalty
also at Bordeaux, as the Duc d'Angoulême is
arrived again, and means to stay a few days before
he goes to join Madame la Duchesse at the Baths
at Vichy. He looks worn, and less calculated than
ever for public shew, but still apparently as amiable
as before. The Duc de G——, though still, I believe, in our 10th Hussars, came in with him, as

his aide-de-camp. The Duc de G—— is come back much disgusted with Paris, and even almost with France and Frenchmen. He says Paris is a dirty place, without society and manners, and that he has met with no one, to whose word, or whose honour, he would fairly trust; that all seemed to be a system of deception and falsehood, and that unless things mend, and alter considerably, he should feel almost disposed, in case of any unfortunate quarrel with England, to renounce France, rejoin his regiment, and become an Englishman. This, I conclude, is the depression of first feelings, which, in the case of emigrants, must be very strong just now. Matters have not quite proceeded to their tastes, and they must, every hour, meet with that which must inevitably disgust them.

We have now also at Bordeaux the celebrated Mademoiselle Georges, the actress from Paris, and Mons. Joami, from the same place. In spite of the heat, I have been three times to hear them in Voltaire's plays, *Mérope, Phèdre,* and *l'Orphelin de la Chine.* The man has neither much figure, nor countenance, and I should only place him as a second-rate performer, though still very superior to the ordinary set here in that line; in fact there are no tragic performers here at all, and the inferiority, beneath mediocrity, with which every other part is sustained, takes off the interest with which these tragedies would be otherwise attended.

Mdlle. Georges herself is also in many parts deficient, both in good taste and in true nature. She is of a large figure, but now fallen to pieces; and I am rather surprised that the *ci-devant* Emperor should have fancied her anywhere except during his Moscow campaign. The story, however, goes here, that at one of their interviews, Bonaparte was taken ill, and in her confusion and ignorance Mdlle. Georges rang the Empress's bell instead of that for the attendants, and that on the arrival of Marie Louise there was of course a scene.

Mdlle. Georges' voice is good, and her countenance would by many be considered fine. In some parts of her acting I think she is strikingly great, but generally forced and extravagant. She runs into extremes from crying to laughing, and from low ghost-like intonations to loud vulgar screams. Upon the whole one comes away fatigued from one of these representations, and not much pleased or affected. And what convinces me that

it really is inferiority in the drama, or in the
actress; and that it is not merely the difference of
style and manner, and national feeling as to com-
position and taste that causes this, is, that you
never see the French part of the audience affected
like an English one, under the influence of really
fine acting. You never hear the generally sup-
pressed sobs, or see the eyes full of tears all round
the house as with us at an English tragedy; when,
for example, Mrs. Siddons plays, and every one
goes away with a serious impression. You only
hear in the French auditors bursts of " *très beau,
très beau, superbe! magnifique!*" &c.; and these
always applied to some extravagant and sudden
change of tone or manner. And now (at this
present writing) if there happens to be a royal
sentiment that can be applied, it is encored like a
song. No one seems carrried away by feelings
which he cannot command; but the applause is
given as it would be to a mountebank for a clever
trick. The distressed heroine or empress spits in
her pocket-handkerchief, or on the stage in the true
French style, and certainly not in a manner to
excite admiration or interest, or to impress the

spectators very strongly with ideas of her dignity and elegance.

The first night the Duc d'Angoulême was at the play (on his arrival here this time), we had verses and songs in his honour, and "*Vive Henri IV.'s*" without end. At last came for once "God save the King," but received very differently from what it was even when first I came here—coolly and civilly enough, except by a few—and I believe we have a few sincere friends here.

As Paris gave a sword to General Sacken, Bordeaux is to give one to Lord Dalhousie; and I really think the town has (as they certainly ought to have) some feelings of gratitude towards him, for his attention to everything that can be of service to the city, and in successful efforts to preserve order, and prevent any mischief being done to the inhabitants. It will be a curious heir-loom in the Dalhousie family, this sword given to their ancestor by the French civil authorities of Bordeaux.

As a trait of the natural French feelings of vanity I may tell you that my loyal patron Mons. Emerigon said, not only should we have been all originally prevented from entering France, had the people been of one mind with the Emperor and the army; but that all along a single word of complaint from Louis XVIII. of the conduct of the allied troops would have been a signal for their entire destruction at any period since.

I am now told that the fifth division, from Bayonne are also on their march to come here to embark, and this will probably cause some little more delay; but I think in ten days we must be on board ship.

Head-Quarters, Bordeaux, July 15th, 1814.— Our final departure from hence appears, at last, to be gradually approaching. The numbers of the English diminish daily; and though we have for this month past been talking of the "next week," I begin to think that another week will really and truly see us off, and the French army again in possession of Bordeaux.

The tradesmen of the town will miss us greatly. They have made a famous time of it these last three months, as the army has in that time received six months pay, and most of it has found its way into the pockets of the keepers of the restaurateurs, the hotels, &c. Bordeaux has had its full share of the spoils of the *milords*. Nor have the inhabitants suffered anything by the army, except the little inconvenience of giving up a room or two in general as quarters for the officers, who partly made up even for this by giving their hosts tickets for the play, taking boxes for the ladies, &c., and making them presents every now and then. The only persons who have suffered by us at all in the neighbourhood, are those who have small gardens, near the camp. They certainly have had their vegetables and fruit gathered gratis, and have generally not even had their share. This evil is, however, exaggerated, and much of it which really exists, has been done by the French peasantry and country servants, who, if a soldier takes six cabbages, immediately take a dozen more themselves, sell them in the camp, and swear to the owners that the soldiers are the culprits.

Those who have vineyards as well as gardens, have also their full revenge in the price of their wines, which were immediately doubled, by the arrival of the troops, and the latter, in fact, pay dearly for their vegetables, though they get a good part for nothing. It is fortunate for the inhabitants that we shall be off before the grapes begin to ripen, and for our own soldiers likewise. Surrounded by vineyards, the temptations would be irresistible, and the means of offence almost boundless; so that the loss to the cultivators of their principal harvest, and the injury to the soldiers, would be very considerable.

I have bought a violoncello to amuse myself this warm weather, and as my host, M. Emerigon, plays the violin in very excellent style, we have frequently music of an evening, before he goes to his consultations.

We most of us, nevertheless, begin to find Bordeaux dull,—I do in particular. My occupation has nearly ceased, except as to swearing the paymasters, &c., to their accounts, &c., and now and then a Court-martial,—not enough to give me full employment, from necessity. The constant expectation of moving, the uncertainty when I may be wanted, and the natural indolence arising from the heat, prevent me from voluntarily engaging in any regular study or pursuit, and even prevent my making any excursions beyond a league or two on my pony. Shut up in this town, which, though airy, as to the general breadth of the streets and openings, is still, in fact, hot and low, and built in a country like that round Woolwich or Deptford, I get thin and languid, and shall be glad to be braced by the sea-air, and the cooler climate of England.

Saturday, 1st.—As yet we have had no packets this week, and being beyond the usual time, this makes us believe the reports which have been some days about, that you mean to send no more packets from England.   I have still hopes.

I must tell you of a trait completely French, of one of the noble guard of honour of the Duc d'Angoulême at Bordeaux.   I had met him twice in the family with whom I live : on one of these occasions, at dinner.   He dined here yesterday, and whilst the rest of the party were taking their coffee, I went to my room to dress, as I dined at Lord Dalhousie's.   This guardsman slipped up stairs after me.   He came bowing into my room, whilst I was in my shirt, and without any excuse or apology, immediately began to tell me he had a little favour to ask, and he hoped that I would oblige him, and say nothing of it in the family, as he would not ask them, and was anxious they should not know anything about it, and at last said, " Could I just let him have five guineas or so, for which he would give me a bit of paper." In short, he added that he was rather deficient in cash, and I should oblige him infinitely by the loan, which should be paid when he could. As I fully expected an application to ask some favour of Lord Dalhousie or the Duke of Wellington, or something very disagreeable, I felt rather relieved by the explanation in full. As he was quite a young man, had just got a commission in the new regiment to be raised in Martinique, and was, I concluded, of good character, from his connection with M. Emerigon and his family, who are held in great esteem, I counted him out his five guineas (all the time in my shirt), and he went away very happy, saying he would go below and leave me a bit of paper, though I told him there was pen and ink in my room. The paper said that he would send Mr. —— six guineas to England (a guinea more than I had given him) as soon as he could. It was signed—*P. de V. De R*——, *De La Martinique*, leaving my name a blank, and not inquiring where he should send, so as to reserve, I presume, enough to satisfy his conscience in not repaying the money, that he should never know where to send it. His bit of paper only confirmed me in my notion that I was doing an act of charity, and not turning Jew or money-lender.

The guard of honour are to-day dismissed, by order of the higher powers from Paris. In truth, there are quite troops enough in France, without adding the expense of these gentlemen, with their white feathers a yard long, and who would be of no use except to quarrel with the regular troops. Only four years since Bonaparte, when at Bordeaux, was attended everywhere by a guard of honour of the same description. Volunteers were his only body-guard.

The Prefêt of Bordeaux last night gave a fête to the Duc d'Angoulême. I went with M. Emerigon. The Duke came a few minutes after eight o'clock in his carriage and six, dressed, I believe, in the uniform of a Field-Marshal, with the *cordon-bleu*, &c. He was received by the Prefêt, attended by Generals Villette, Blagnac, Clement de la Ronciere, &c., and a number of old and new nobility, all in their best; and having been, as it were, proclaimed to the company by the Prefêt, the Duke went about most graciously, talking to every one as usual.

About ten, supper was announced (as the Duke

has very early habits), and in about half an
hour after, he came to the window to see very
pretty fire-works, which were let off in the main
street, surrounded by thousands of people below,
and at all the windows. It was a gay and at-
tractive scene. Soon after eleven the Duke went
home, as he rises at five, and works hard at business, on petitions, &c., and at four o'clock to-
morrow morning is to start for Bayonne. He had
been at two reviews in the course of yesterday,
and had both times been in tolerably severe storms.
I fancy he must now and then wish himself quiet
again, as he has been the last twenty years. I
am almost sure I should. The new barons and
nobility seem to make very good courtiers. Indeed,
the duties are all the same, it is only a change in the
cry and the idol, the same worship exists as before.
There was the Prefêt, Monsieur Le Baron de V——,
while the fire-works were going on, observing to
all around him, loud enough on purpose for the
Duke to hear,—how fortunate he was, to have
thought of the fire-works; that the idea had come
into his head, as he observed every one would see
Monseigneur so well at the window, whilst the fire-
works were going off: and then how plain we

can read the inscriptions—O, yes, observe *Vive le Duc d'Angoulême, Vivent les Bourbons,* and the fleurs-de-lys—how well they look in the midst of the fire! He felt quite happy that he had thought of all this to gratify the people, as it necessarily must do. Now the inscriptions were close to us and in letters a foot long. And note besides, that this Baron was one of the functionaries who ran away from Bordeaux, when the Duke came here on the 12th of March, and who would probably not now have his situation, if my patron and some others had not persuaded him to return in good time, and continue in his office to see the result. The Duke must see through this, and be disgusted.

The women here are not as well dressed as at Toulouse; not so stylish. They do not show as much blood and fashion. I believe, however, among the higher orders, there is much more morality, and that there is a greater difference in reality, as well as in outward appearance, between the ladies in the dress boxes, and those in the tier above, than there was at Toulouse.

By a little after eleven, the few English who were present at the fête, were nearly all gone home, being chiefly Generals and their aides-de-camp. I came away, leaving the company waltzing and dancing away with less spirit and skill than at Toulouse.

I meet with some very liberal Catholics here; for instance, a gentleman said yesterday, before me, that if all the pieces of the true cross were collected, they would, when put together, make a cross half a mile long. A lady in company said to a friend (also before me), that she did not much trouble the father confessor, and indeed, it was what she liked the least of any part of her duty. She added, that their religion depended on faith, hope, and charity, and that she understood (addressing me), ours did so too, but theirs required a good deal of hope. Madame Emerigon, with whom I live, is returned home highly delighted with Paris, but abusing the inhabitants, who she says, think only of making money, taking in strangers, provincials and foreigners, and amusing themselves day and night.

She is a French creole from one of the islands. A little mulatto girl, about fourteen, always stands behind her chair, laughing at all her mistress says. The hairdresser is generally seated in one corner of the room, half the dinner time, joining in the conversation, and sometimes adorning Madame, whilst we are taking our wine, and during this time, an idle Paris lad, of the girl's age, whom Madame seems to have fancied because he speaks such good French, and not the patois, is running about, bustling, but in reality doing little or nothing from morning till night. Three other female servants, and a nephew of the family complete the party on this side of the house, or rather wing.

In an opposite wing, are, first, in the upper part, two respectable old ladies, and their servants; below them, *au premier*, is an old West Indian gentleman, and his two sons, both *ci-devant* of the imperial guard of honour from Bordeaux, and his two daughters, with servants, &c. None of these are very elegant, nor, as far as I can judge from one visit, very well bred. They amused me the whole time with talking of the superiority of the French troops, and how the Imperial Guards in particular, could beat all the Allies if not more than two to one, as they always had done, &c., to which I could only say that I believed the Imperial Guards had been all withdrawn from the army of Spain, at least I supposed so, and that I had had, therefore, no opportunity of judging. One Miss also asked what the English lived upon? as she understood we ate no bread;—upon which a French visitor, to save me the trouble of explanation, informed her that we principally lived upon *des potates* (which is now the word here for potatoes) and *bétraves*, with which accurate information she seemed quite satisfied. This sort of conversation, and a few songs quite in the French style, which I do not at all admire, though one of the demoiselles had a good voice, have not tempted me to pay another visit.

The other night I went to the benefit of Madame Georges. She acted Semiramis, in Voltaire's play, and with considerable success, particularly when she let nature have its way. She also acted in the sentimental farce of *La Belle Fermière*, and really well, if she had but omitted a miserable song accompanied by an old violin or two behind the scenes, all out of tune. The orchestra as well as every part of the house was full—every passage almost crammed near the openings to the boxes. The play began at seven o'clock, and the company were all ready by four, and I saw many well-dressed women going to the play at two and three o'clock, as a box cannot be engaged without paying almost double price. The Duke was very well received, and as there was luckily no band, we escaped about five and twenty *Vive Henri IV's,* which we should otherwise have had.

Mr. Wilberforce should exert himself in getting little essays written in French on the slave trade, circulated in France, to enlighten the people in some degree at least. At present, even the more intelligent and better sort of men seem only to consider the English as playing the part of Don Quixote in this business, and consider the whole as a sort of romantic affectation of humanity; whilst many others insinuate motives not quite so honourable, by stating that having well supplied our own islands with slaves, we wish to give up all the other colonies, with a diminished black population, and in bad condition, and then to prevent their ever recovering themselves. This is to be done by the abolition of the Slave Trade; whilst our own islands, in full prosperity, will be ready to reap the benefit of the distress of their rivals.

July 18*th.*—I have now only time to seal up and to tell you I have nothing new to add, except that the returns of embarkations are just arrived from Pouillac, by which it appears that all the troops are now actually on board, except the two brigades of Guards, one of which entered Pouillac to-day to be prepared, and the other is still here. At present no more shipping is ready, though more are expected, some say we shall be moving about to-morrow week, some this day fortnight; but I believe no one knows anything of the matter.

From the following entry in the Diary kept by Mrs. Larpent, it appears that Mr. F. S. Larpent arrived at his father's house at East Sheen on the 8th August, 1814.

8th August, 1814.

" In the evening came Seymour, looking younger than when he went away, and in excellent health, after having been absent two years all but a fortnight. We thanked God sincerely for this great mercy and happiness."

APPENDIX.

APPENDIX I.

LETTER referred to at Page 95, Vol. II.

Head-Quarters, September 4, 1813.

DEAR SIR,

I WAS very much concerned to hear of your misfortune, which, however, I don't doubt will have been alleviated by the Comte Gazan as far as may have been in his power, as soon as he will have known that to your humanity, in the first instance, he owed the safety of his wife.

In former wars a person in your situation would have been considered a non-combatant, and would have been immediately released ; but in this war, which, on account of the violence of enmity in which it is conducted, it is to be hoped will be the last, for some time at least, everybody taken is considered a prisoner of war, and none are released without exchange. There are several persons now in my power in the same situation with yourself in that respect, that is to say, non-combatants according to the known and anciently practised rules of war ; among others, there is the Secretary of the Governor of St. Sebastian, and I authorise you to tell the Duke of Dalmatia or the Count Gazan that I will send back any person in exchange for you that they will point out.

I send you, with this letter, the sum of two hundred dollars, of which I request you to acknowledge the receipt, and that you will let me know whether I can do anything else for you.

Ever yours, most faithfully,

WELLINGTON.

F. Seymour Larpent, Esq.

APPENDIX II.

[Although the annexed letter does not come chronologically within the scope of Mr. Larpent's Journal, as there is an anticipatory notice towards the close of the Third Volume, of Sir John Murray's trial, it may not inappropriately be inserted here.]

Paris, January 19th, 1815.

MY DEAR SIR,

IN regard to Sir John Murray's trial, I intended to prove the charges framed by my directions against him, in consequence of the orders of Government, by the production of my Instructions and his Reports, all of which are in the Government Offices.

Sir John Murray contends that one paragraph of my Instructions directed him not to risk an action. I think he has mistaken my meaning in that paragraph; but whether he has or not, that paragraph did not recall the other Instructions for his conduct.

The object of that paragraph was to prevent the Spanish Generals Elio and the Duque del Parque, from taking advantage of Sir John Murray's absence, and the temporary command which they had of the cavalry belonging to Sir John Murray's and Whittingham's corps to attack the French. There existed a prevailing opinion among the Spanish officers that their failures were to be attributed to the want of good cavalry; and this paragraph of the Instructions was drawn with the view of preventing those officers from attempting to fight a general action when circumstances should have placed a small body of good cavalry at their disposal, more particularly as all the manœuvres ordered by the Instructions had in view to prevent the necessity of a general action.

I have not by me the Instructions, but, as well as I recollect, this meaning of the paragraph is obvious; and it will be particularly observed that it comes in after the directions for the formation of the corps Romain in Bohemia with the Duque del Parque and General Elio. I think, as I before stated, that this paragraph has nothing to say to the question of Sir John Murray's guilt or innocence of the two charges, though it has to that brought against him by the Admiral.

The Court has, of course, a right to judge of my meaning by the words in which it is conveyed, in whatever manner I may now explain it or you may explain it for me, as the obvious meaning of those words was to be the guide of Sir John Murray's conduct. I must add also, that whatever care I may have taken, it is not improbable that in drawing an Instruction for the operations of so many corps, all with separate Commanders-in-Chief, I may not in every instance have made use of the language which should convey the meaning I had in my mind.

There is nothing else that occurs to me; but I shall be glad to hear from you occasionally during the trial, and receive a copy of the evidence when it can be got.

Believe me,
Ever yours, most faithfully,

WELLINGTON.

To F. S. Larpent, Esq..
&c.   &c.

LONDON:

Printed by Schulze and Co., 13 Poland Street.

Printed in Great Britain by
Amazon.co.uk, Ltd.,
Marston Gate.